GARDEN OF EXPERIENCE

BY

: MRS. CRAN :

WITH 16 ILLUSTRATIONS
FROM PHOTOGRAPHS
TAKEN BY THE AUTHOR

HERBERT JENKINS LIMITED
3 YORK STREET ST. JAMES'S
LONDON S.W. 1 ❀ ❀ MCMXXII

A
HERBERT
JENKINS'
BOOK

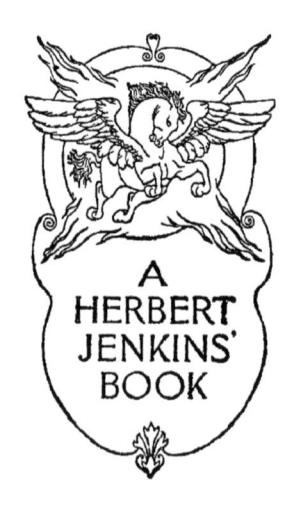

The Mayflower Press, Plymouth, England. William Brendon & Son, Ltd:

TO LESLEY

IN MEMORY OF OUR FIGHTS AND MISTAKES

OUR QUARRELS AND OUR TEARS

OF OUR KISSES AND OUR LAUGHTER, OUR FORGIVINGS

AND ADVENTURINGS

IN MEMORY OF ALL THOSE THINGS WHICH

MAKE UP OUR HAPPY LOVE

FOREWORD

> . . . Go, little book, and wish to all
> Flowers in the garden, meat in the hall,
> A bin of wine, a spice of wit,
> A house with lawns enclosing it. . . .
>   R. L. STEVENSON.

SOME time ago I wrote a book called *The Garden of Ignorance*. It was not the textbook of an expert, but the expression of an enthusiasm I could not control and must needs share with my fellow-humans—the overflow of a vast and flowing joy. For years I had been bond slave to London, and some need, of which I was only half aware, drove me constantly, whenever I had a holiday or could snatch a weekend, into the country, to the gardens of friends, to lone woodlands or remote hamlets, to any place where flowers grew.

I did not know that an instinct stronger than myself was driving me into the great arms of Nature; but with each assuagement came a deeper craving for more and more of her comforting, till, at last, the wheel of fortune revolved for me three acres of sandy soil on a pine-set Surrey hill.

Never could woman have looked upon her kingdom with sheerer ignorance than I! I did not know a rhododendron from a laurel. I had no inkling that this shaggy stretch of unkempt soil held all the magic and mystery of the priestly vows I soon must take. For soon I bent my knee to Mother Earth; laid my hands in her dear hands, and consecrated all the best of me to her service in the garden on the hill—I turned from the hurt of cities to Nature—turned my cheek to her buffeting winds, my heart to her laughing stars.

And out of this gladness I wrote a book for any to read who care to know where joy bubbles fresh from an inexhaustible spring. It was a book for beginners who have not yet worn the yoke of technical garden terms; full of questing effort and boundless faith; brimful of the stumbling wonder and laughter in the heart of a child when it turns over the edge of Never-was into the exciting realities of Time. I was a child in the nursery of the wise old mother, her great arms folded me when I came to their clasp at last; my head was near her heart as I crept into the shelter of her terrible patience; it will never leave that place again as long as I live; nor after, except to creep up closer.

It was a laughing, merry, useless book, written in the careless days of peace before 1914, and the public was very kind to it; so kind to its many

FOREWORD

faults that the Editor of *The Gentlewoman* asked me to write a series of articles upon the same garden, from the lowly crag of experience to which I have so far climbed upon the mountain of a gardener's efforts. Some of these are here, with my obeisance to him for his kind permission.

The title is a lordly one, here and now let me say that all my real experience after fifteen years of happy gardening is the bitter sweet of learning how less than nothing I do know, and all the wisdom I can claim is that my feet are set among the flowers which spring from the mystery-miracle of my own setting in the magic hands of Earth. Those things I have gained, and also a deep sweet draught of gladness from the wells of friendship. How closely and how kindly a garden knits the bond of friends.

Readers have covered me with confusion from time to time by fancying my garden plot is a large estate. I repeat with nauseating diligence whenever opportunity occurs that I have but three acres—and even those, these days, are ragged and torn with the rough years of war; but they always believe that I am only being humble, and persist in picturing not the garden I have, but the garden I dream I will have. The latter is more real to me than any mortal pleasaunce could ever be, but most people are very literal and in the light of fact are apt to look upon the dreamer as a liar—God help them. Yet, come to think of it, the dreamers may take heart of grace ; for to the eternal honour of our generation—*The Yellow Jacket* has been produced !

I have seen life from many angles ; touched it at many points ; and nothing it has offered has given me more lasting joy than the song of the wind in pine trees or the thin light of stars upon the roses after rain. Not all the glamour of ardent London life, not all the impact of the surge of civilisation in the tidal boom of days has brought me so much of sweetness, or so near to courage, as the patient toil in my garden.

There I have fingered the pulse of Time, beating in great rhythms of day and night; watched the sap-tide surge up from the soil in spring ; flow in the summer ; and sink back to earth in the autumn ; felt the pendulum of the seasons swing from side to side of the globe, and so leaned with this little vibrant atom of life, which is me, on the structure of the Universe.

As I eased off from the first long thirsty drink at the well of Earth-Life, to take a deep breath and look on the things around, I found I was one of a vast community of happy souls, set in a whole world of lovely gardens. Never a lane in this our Britain but had its cot surrounded by flowers and fruit ; never an ancient wall but grew a clinging robe of ivy, clematis or wistaria ; never a mellow misty evening but heard the tempered clang of spade and fork, those bell notes of the dusk which every peasant rings for his home curfew.

I awakened to a new kingdom; the farm-labourers, the railwaymen, the tradesmen, the gasworks men, the mechanics of the country town sauntered home at evening to ply their native skill in the strip of garden about their cottages. This one was the best grower of peas, this one had a passion for violas, this knew something of topiary work, and left his mark on many a yew tree and box-hedge in the neighbourhood, and yet another would win the palm for roses far and wide. These remote, unknown, silent men had a sweetness at the heart which I had never guessed at heretofore; they were brother-priests with me in service.

The beauty of my Land which I had hitherto accepted as a part of it, God-sent and predestined, was due, I found, to the loving service of generations of beauty-lovers; quiet peasant toil in hours of scanty leisure had furnished the length and breadth of the Island with quaint and beautiful gardens; and in turning myself to win to beauty from the wild a patch of Surrey sand, I had only come into line with my Race, and obeyed the call of the blood.

Having suffered the extreme of desire, I feel therefore the most real sympathy with all who would have and have not a garden. To them I speak. To them I say—get one. Make a way to the heart's need.

You who yearn for the first and the last and the best Religion, without knowing how great and good your desires are, get you to the arms of our Mother and taste peace.

CONTENTS

CHAPTER		PAGE
	FOREWORD	7
I.	THE FLOWER SHOW	17
II.	NEW SCHOOL-BOOKS	36
III.	PERSONALITIES IN A GARDEN	49
IV.	"AWE-TIME" AND THE BULBOUS HOUR	68
V.	THE HOOLIGAN AND THE PICNIC	79
VI.	FLOWERS FAR OFF	105
VII.	BEE-CRAFT	136
VIII.	THE KINGDOM OF PAN	167
IX.	RAIN ON THE HERBS	188
X.	THE FORTUNE-TELLER	209
XI.	ROSES	227
XII.	THE WOOING OF TATTY-BOGLE	242
XIII.	JAM AND THE COOK-POTS	262
XIV.	LOVERS IN THE GARDEN	279
XV.	DROUGHT IN THE GARDEN	287
XVI.	HALLOW E'EN	303

ILLUSTRATIONS

"A sailor-man of high degree"	*Frontispiece*
	PAGE
"The bird yard—and in the distance the crooked old plum-tree in a tiled path"	19
"The portrait"	41
"Her picture of the wood and hammocks"	41
"The American passed across the garden-life like a cyclone, leaving behind him splendid new hives"	53
"The cottage; deep-set in pine and bracken, where the Hooligan makes merry with bones"	81
"Shorn of her plaits"	127
"The peppermint rock long since sucked away, and its owner a soldierly cadet!"	127
"As they passed over each cottage the village folk came out to cry and marvel"	153
"The long hair interfered with her play"	159
"Dandy likes drinking from the bird-bath better than from his own bowl"	159
"Domino, the spotted kid"	181
"The war baby . . . Over our tender task we re-modelled the world. . . ."	181
"The flagged garden in summer-time, where a tall tree accents the scene"	195
"The lead boy and the flagged garden in early spring"	201
"To-night is the night of the dead"	231
"Tatty-Bogle let out a piercing yell"	257
"He espied the coquette smirking among the bushes"	257
"A figure of wrath, strangely like a jackal"	257
"Digging the holes for planting roses"	267
"The picking of jam-fruit is the excuse for many a happy day"	267
"Making the goats' milking-stool"	289
"Better here, in the wan moonlight—the valley below swimming full of mist"	305

THE GARDEN OF EXPERIENCE

CHAPTER I

THE FLOWER SHOW

> . . . He does not die that can bequeath
> Some influence to the land he knows,
> Or dares, persistent, interwreath
> Love permanent with the wild hedgerows;
>   He does not die, but still remains
>   Substantiate with his darling plains. . . .
> HILAIRE BELLOC.

TREES can hold one's heart. The little tender flowers come and go; but trees abide and fill the years like friendship, or like Fate.

We lost a tree once, and the gap it left behind taught us more than anything else could have done how great a hold it had taken upon our hearts; and from that awakening we grew to look upon the rest of our trees with love-sharpened eyes, counting them over in new appreciation; the silver birch in front of the "parlour" window which makes lace-work for us against the sky in winter, and a pattern like maidenhair-fern when its pale green buds peep in spring; the tall Thuja which stands like an exclamation point against the blue-grey distance of the valley; the great squirrel and owl-haunted Beech, away down at the bottom of the kitchen garden; the Quince tree we planted a dozen years ago, growing in leaf shades of silver grey, and bearing golden-perfumed fruit; the crimson May upon the lawn which was planted by two of the " family " before they went pioneering out West almost as long ago as the Quince, and which we solemnly know (though we do not ask any outsider to believe us) grows richly the years either of them is coming home to see us, and droops when they or theirs fare ill. It tells news of them, times, before they do themselves.

The old plum tree was a character; a knotted misshapen, grumbling besom, growing in the middle of a red-tiled path where the crankiness of its shape became dear to us, as well as its snowstorm of blossom in spring and its treasure of dark purple plums in autumn. It had had a cruel childhood we knew from its twisted back and scowling face, but its heart was sweet and generous towards us; and the birds dwelt peacefully in its thick branches.

One windy winter morning some of the bedroom windows were a little too light, and a part of the

"The bird yard;—and in the distance the crooked old plum-tree in a tiled path." *Chap. I.*

lawn a great deal too dark; our old witch-wife had been blown down while we slept, and great was her fall. We missed our plum tree; it left a gap in the garden pictures; with the spring we mourned for the lost blossoming, and later bewailed the purple fruit.

One day, wheeling a barrow of loam along the red-tiled path, now so pitifully clear of its hump-backed nuisance, I saw a ghost. Right in the path lay a round ripe purple plum; just one single plum, exactly like the hundreds we had been wont to harvest yearly in that very spot; I picked it up; it wore the silvery blue bloom upon its purple skin which we had always admired so much in the fruit of our lost tree. I tasted it, the same sweet cool, juicy refreshment, the same golden flesh.

I looked around—peering at me over the bracken and bramble a few yards away was the child of our plum tree, watching me taste its firstling. A little young baby witch, with an even more crooked back than its misshapen mother, having struggled for lone hard years to the stage of fruit-bearing through the malicious strangling envious hands of bramble and gorse in the ill-lighted suburbs of the pine wood.

How it ever collected sense and strength to throw its ewe-plumling at my feet I do not know; I suppose ancestry counts for something and there was wizardry about the parentage for sure.

I hurried to proclaim this great news, and the family ran to survey and rejoice in the marvel. A couple of months later I assisted the girl-gardener to prepare a comfortable place for the little tree, close by the old tiled path ; and there it now grows quietly and confidently, dearly loved by all of us, because we never look on its features but we remember its grim old mother whose heart was greater than her deformity, and who died in harness game to the last. The youngster gives us a few purple plums year by year ; and some day, maybe, we shall see its spreading branches offer sanctuary to tit and starling, chaffinch and thrush, as its mother's did of old.

I never see a well-grown Malus, but I think of a weather-beaten old gentleman who had one and loved it well. He had been a sailor once, and now was tethered to the unyielding land by age and rheumatism, his wife dead, his children spread far and wide. In his loneliness he turned to a little garden for healing and for comradeship, groaning grievously as he bent his stiffened knees about his work.

In the middle of his small lawn was a beautiful young standard *Malus Floribundi*, upon which he lavished the most thoughtful attentions. Year by year it spread a gloriously wider shade, year by year it broke into a wider wonder of pink flushed bloom ; and passing his garden gate I would regard him sitting smoking his evening pipe, watching it with an air of rich content.

During the war certain restless spirits busied themselves telling everyone else what to do; and I heard such an one waylay our mariner on an evening, something after this style.

"You'll be digging up your grass and growing food like the rest of us, Mr. Matheson? And what a pity your nice crab will have to go, such a pity . . . but then the Nation needs food and we can none of us study luxuries."

Pompous priggish words, cruel and senseless. I trembled lest he might be persuaded to root up his pride and comfort for the sustenance of his, or any other, vile body. But the sturdy old seafarer had too much sense to try and turn his tiny patch of ground into a carrot or potato bed, though the "patriot" had certainly poisoned his pride and peace. Thereafter his air was more like that of a tiger defending its young than a weary old man enjoying an amiable hobby. His embittered eye would peer through the hedge at every approaching footstep, and his peaceful preoccupied days wholly changed by an irritable restlessness. He was always on wrathful guard lest some new-comer would appear to repeat the hideous words.

When Armistice muted all the guns in Europe I saw him again in the demi-light of a pale November dawn mightily busy, groaning once more with all his old vigour over spade and trowel, the beloved Malus swaying exultantly over his labour. Life for him had resumed its sweetness, and my heart, unknown, was sweetened by the sight.

With the return of peace to the riven days I also abandoned myself gleefully to flower-indulgence, making yearly pilgrimage to the Mecca of the Chelsea Flower Show, with intensified pleasure. The last one found me incommoded, if flattered, by the company of a Playwright, whose handsome person was adorned like Solomon's self in magnificent apparel, and who speedily proved to be much more interested in the social throng than in the exhibits; a conflict of desires, therefore, naturally rose between us; for while I wanted to dawdle in the tents, consulting catalogues and experts, he regarded the whole affair as a magnified garden-party and preferred to sun himself in the smiles and badinage of the many brilliant acquaintances who sped like meteors through the grounds.

Being but female, and humble at that, I was speedily swallowed up in his dominant will; my waggon was hitched to his star, and I led a life of unwonted social splendour, till it occurred to me to get lost; and craftily seizing a moment when he was engrossed with a Duke I crept behind some peacocks carved in box and yew, and thence back to a tent where I had seen a display of handsome new irises. Here I sloughed the skins of shyness and unease, becoming an ardent happy human being, thankful to find myself near flowers again.

Among the Oriental Poppies in the garden at home is a lovely thing of great white petals blotted at the base with dark purple, near by it grows a flaunting flirting pink, and we always call them "Perry and his Missis," because we know the white is called Perry's White, and we feel sure the twain are related in some close bonds because they both have the purple patch at the heart. I was therefore interested to notice that the gorgeous display of irises to which I had wended my stolen way, came from one Perry's Hardy Plant Farm, and looked round to see if my old married friends were there. Sure enough, I presently saw a great bowl of the white poppy, patch and all complete, so I knew that I had tracked him to his birthplace, and greeted his familiar old face with a grin I trust no one saw but himself.

The irises filled me with avaricious joy, for there was a superb collection of the new rhizomatous varieties which grow kindly on the hot soil of our Surrey hill. Remembering Mr. Zwanny's early flowering I bethought me to enquire if all these were naturally abloom, or whether they had been retarded or forced for Show; an important matter for the trusting amateur who desires to compound new colour-schemes for the garden.

I told the story of Mr. Zwanny's untoward appearance in the bed he was expected to adorn, and learned from a salesman whom I remember for his pleasant enthusiasm, that every exhibit had come from the open ground and could be trusted to bloom as now ; as well as to produce the same strong stems, some four feet high, carrying six or seven of the banner-like flowers.

Refreshed by this pleasing information I plunged headlong into the intoxication of ordering a purple bed to range alongside the blue one where Irises Pallida, Victor and Beatrice queen it among Anchusa and Catmint, Campanula and Delphinium.

It was a glorious hour, full of the tingling joy of the truant schoolboy, in which the voice of economy was hushed and my deserted escort utterly forgotten. The body of the new bed was to be the dark velvety purple lupin Zulu, with some Fireflame and Captain lupins to sharpen the colour ; and among these the lordly irises Alcazar, Lady Sackville, Isolene, Seedling Ninety-Two, Prosper Languier, and Cherubin, would plead with, and point, the throbbing purple scheme . . . dainty little Iris Tenax clamouring about their knees.

The enthusiast who booked this order was pleased with the grouping, and told me that this race of superb irises had taken fifteen years of careful work to produce, coming mainly through a Pallida and Trojana cross. A very beautiful variety is Lady

THE FLOWER SHOW

Sackville, she has purple falls, bronze-netted at the base where the lady flaunts a long blonde moustache; her standards are pale lilac—feminine to a degree. For the border of this bed I told myself that Aubretia Doctor Mules would make a glowing ribbon, and the feathered Muscari, a pale heliotrope, soften the transition upward to Tenax.

I had the bit well between my teeth by this time, and set off hotfoot to find some long-desired standard gooseberry, apple and damson trees, passing bewildering masses of azaleas, rhododendrons, roses and cinerarias on the way; with my goal in sight I fell right into the arms of the Playwright who, lost in a maze of abject apologies, remorsefully conducted me to tea and ices, to the great loss of the garden.

I wandered next day down to the orchard to consider how I might make amends for failing to choose and order the young trees on which I set my heart, and spent most of the day waylaid by imagination, wondering instead of working, for which I had to pay later by an attack of conscience. Some of the fruit trees obviously needed root-pruning, and I was trying to decide which to start upon when my mental eye went wandering down the searchlight ray of wonder to the paralysis of more practical affairs. I became conscious of that vast underworld, upon the surface of which we scrape and scratch so confidently in the pursuit of what we call gardening.

Scrambling away from every tree I saw myriads of tiny mouths, each making with absolute surety for the direction where food is to be found. How do these little groping fibres know the way to go? They always creep, uncannily prescient, towards food. I was mesmerised, with a vision of the communal life of this world of roots. The big roots are pillars of society; they stretch powerful arms into the soil and take a grip strong enough to bear the tree up above in the light and air; arms strong enough to face any equinoctial gale; and then there are the thousands of tiny annual radiculæ, fibrous rootlets, which live their little lives from spring to autumn and are the most valuable of all; intelligent little travellers who wander far and wide from their first anchorage in the search for means of support for the rollicking *bon viveur* above.

As these fibres die off in winter it is time to transplant and root-prune the trees which have too much wood and too little fruit before the heavy frosts. When the little myriad mouths are in full cry after food during spring and summer the shock to the tree of any disturbance would be too great. The quiescence of late autumn is the time for operation. Whatever produces an excessive development of root prevents the production of seed; and this knowledge has been a boon to growers of fruit trees, because many of them are conscious of that phenomenon in their midst, a healthy, not to say robust, fruit tree—which will make young shoots nearly a yard long—which will even further exasperate by bursting into laterals from shoots of the same season, in such rude health is the whole tree, but yet will not produce anything approaching an adequate crop of fruit or even blossom.

If about a third of the roots are cut away, that is to say, of ends of the roots (leaving the fibrous mat) and replanted on a properly constructed station of clinker stone, etc., the result is extraordinary. The treatment checks the formation of leaf-buds and encourages blossom buds. A tree so treated should subsequently be encouraged to form surface roots by a system of mulching. It seems a hard bed for them to lie on, but there is sense in the idea, for it secures drainage and also forms a kind of hard pavement which forces the trees to throw out horizontal roots.

I always feel pleased to find a fruit tree that has grown insolent and lazy on too much luxury, the cure for swollen head in an orchard is so simple and so sure. It is much more grateful work than trying to cure diseased and neglected trees. My tiny orchard was badly planted in the days of impatience and ignorance. It rebukes me when I go near it, and earns me, sometimes, a sorrowful glance from the lass I love. Under my light hot soil is iron sandstone, and the young trees were planted over that, with no substratum of rammed brick to keep the roots horizontal and prevent them from boring into that most unkind entertainment. The results are plain to see in the scarred split bark and ne'er-do-weel habits of the unfortunate nurslings.

Pears will grow joyously on any kind of soil that has a dry subsoil. Peaches also insist upon a sound, dry subsoil; but they are more cranky than the genial-hearted pears, and will sicken and sulk on deep, damp rich borders. Besides shallow planting and light soil an essential accompaniment to successful peach-growth is thorough top-dressing every spring, about May.

Have any readers amused themselves by growing young orchards for themselves from pear and apple pips? Apple seeds, nice ripe brown ones out of some choice favourite varieties, should be planted in autumn, choosing the largest and fattest pips. They may be planted one inch deep and six inches apart each way. At the end of the first year they can be put out of the pots or border (which should have been of light rich loam) into nursery rows one foot apart each way, and a year later planted where they are to produce fruit not less than eight feet apart every way. They can be induced to fruit in four or five years if first encouraged to great luxuriance of growth, then lifted and severely root-pruned, taking care to prune away all tap, or forked, roots and using every means to encourage surface fibres. The less pruning of

THE FLOWER SHOW

the shoots the better, as the knife is a great enemy to early fruitfulness in young trees.

This method of growing apples is more exciting than raising them from cuttings or by grafting, as one never knows exactly what kind of apple one is growing from seed. There is a pleasant sensation of gambling, in the game, one throws the dice with Nature, and though the wait is a long one every orchardist learns how to practise patience before he may gather his fruit. Pear pips should be sown in February.

One of the nicest peaches I ever tasted came to our garden in this seedling way. My father, an ardent gardener, took me when very young to a flower show, and I trotted after him through the steamy tents all through a hot afternoon with great goodwill. I loved him very well, and it was worth a lot of leg-ache to see the gorgeous flowers that excited him so much. However, I lost him in due course (as I had often feared I would during the strenuous rounds) so retired under a fruit-laden trestle, where I presently fell asleep on a vast discarded pumpkin.

At twilight I was ferreted out, much refreshed, to meet the Pater's conscience-stricken eye; a kindly prize-winner, who had helped him in his long search for me, comforted us each with an illustrious first-prize peach. Father, full of gloomy self-rebuke, took his home; but I lapped mine up in much haste, and buried the stone in a comely spot under a southern wall, on the way home, in the drive. Father made a hole for it with his stick, and five years later it bore its first fruit. It may be there now full of years and honours for all I know ; it certainly throve well, and did us very proud as long as we remained in the old house.

Nut trees are interesting ; sometimes one finds that the filbert trees have female blossoms, with few or no catkins. A very important matter, because there will be no crops unless the pollen is brought within reach. It is not everyone who knows the appearance of filbert *debutantes*. They are so modest. But they are well worth troubling to see. Look down the branches of your filbert trees and you will see on many of the fat buds a tiny, almost microscopic crimson fringe. A tassel of red so wee it is like a secret that the bush is trying to hide. It is the lady filbert. Swinging about, very debonair in the breeze, should be bunches of lambstails or catkins, the handsome young knights of the nut tree on the look-out for adventure.

As their bridal hour approaches they burst out in a glory of golden dust, which the wind scatters upon the shy little scarlet fringes demurely waiting the magic moment. And lo ! in Nature's appointed hour a good crop of nuts. But if one finds a large number of fringed beauties and a piteously small display of gallants, it is politic to go into the woods and choose branches full of catkins at the time when the gold dust is just beginning to burst, it does not matter what variety, probably the wild hazel is best, and tie these branches high up among the bushes most needing them; they should be tied high so that the Danæ-shower may fall upon the crimson tassels below.

Talking of planting fruit trees reminds me of the fun it is to study the different varieties of digging; there is the laborious conscientious spade which toils industriously through the soil, turning up mechanically and without love dull brown clods which are—to surer vision—a miraculous laboratory full of mystery and power. Then there is the feverish worker, even worse than the first, who tosses the earth aside in paroxysms of irregular energy, seeing nothing and achieving little more; blind undirected force working in a furious unrest.

Then there is the real digger; the mellowed, leisured, thorough workman; who, be he squire or hind, dame or maid, is all poet to the soil. He breathes with the earth as it exhales. His spade is a sacred helpmate in a ceremonious rite—not a clumsy unpresentable sign of degrading toil—it is kept bright as a soldier's sword, and in his hand is sensitive as a maid in love to every variation of the soil.

The digger of fine mental quality with imagination

and patience who notices every creeping creature uncovered by his digging, and feels his way delicately as a surgeon among the fibrous roots, is using his spade as a conductor between himself and the earth. He—a bundle of love, intelligence and energy—and the earth a mine of mysterious wonderful force; the two made one by a spade! As one grows older one learns over and over again, till the lesson is indelibly graven, that in ourselves is poverty or riches, gain or loss, beauty or squalor. Everything is in personality.

There is one blessed thing about this garden work—it is brim full of legend and tradition and romance. Even manures are romantic, properly regarded. Look back on the tale of garden ingenuity and see the marvels we have won from the wild. Progressing by infinitesimal degrees culture has worked magic wonders improbable as any childish fairy-tale; it has taken rustic nobodies from hedge and cliff and sand-dune, planted them in rich and luxurious environment, tended them with thoughtful patience, propagated them with stern selection, till we have all the radiant train of summer roses from the frail hoyden of our hedgerows; the deep-fleshed, close-woven, great-hearted cabbage from the long-stalked, scanty-leaved, ill-smelling wildling growing on the ocean cliffs; and the great white purple-tipped sticks of asparagus from a wiry spindle found among the dunes.

One could elaborate the list to infinity; it is brim full of incidents and gentle history. The triumphs of the gardeners who have passed before us are the lighted lamps we take pride in passing on to the gardeners who will come after us.

CHAPTER II

NEW SCHOOL-BOOKS

> Prim little scholars are the flowers of her garden,
> Trained to stand in rows, and asking if they please.
> I might love them well but for loving more the wild ones:
> O my wild ones! They tell me more than these. . . .
>
> GEORGE MEREDITH.

I AM never sure if I am an iconoclast or a pioneer. But I *am* quite sure that a lot of my sentiment towards life, as ordained and lived in my generation, is destructive. There are a number of things I hate. The hate springs from a sense of discomfort. Whenever I find myself pitchforked, through no fault of my own, into an environment which bores or disgusts me, I look around for the reason of the trouble, and hate it—hate it actively, with the gloves on.

One of the things I have hated all my life has been the yawns of my childhood. People say, " It was the happiest time of your life . . . look back and say if it was not." . . . Indulgently and sloppily they try to lure me into an untrue admission. For it was not the happiest time of my life at all. I was never happy till I could do as I liked; and that was long, long after childhood.

When I look back on my first decade and a half on this globe I am chiefly conscious of yawning hours of grievous and pitiful boredom. My parents were kind beyond the average, fond and serious; but they, poor souls, were deeply involved in the problems of finance attendant on the rearing of a large family on a very small income, and so could necessarily spare little time for the niceties of observation and analysis of their babes' psychology.

They suspected me of some intelligence and strained their tiny powers—dear and devoted twain—to send me to a large school run on old-fashioned and unprogressive lines, where I speedily learned to hate incessantly and bitterly the world to which I found myself born.

I was large; active; constantly urged from within by a spring of energy; bitten with an observant experimental brain; and of all unfortunate gifts for a child in such a humdrum not to say sordid walk in life, the whole bend and bias of my temperament was romantic.

Penned within the classroom walls, my young limbs chafed to be abroad and moving; uttering the Catechism daily, in common with a hundred other girls with hands folded behind our backs, I dreamed of a future day when I would discard all

Catechisms and sing poems to the ravishment of the great world. With reluctant fingers closing over a slate pencil, I would chase the crabbed adventures of one " X," while I itched to remember that the lucky gipsies out on the wide roadway under the lofty sky might turn their brown hands to the comelier task of weaving willow wands or making brooms.

Little reliefs came my way now and again, which were not after all so much reliefs as a blinding glimpse of what life could be. The drawing mistress came to our class one term with twenty tiny boxes. In each were a row of colours and a brush . . . twenty pair of eyes bent curiously on the phenomena, and one at least eyed the clear paints with throbbing and devouring greed. I believe colour has always made me drunk . . . and when we were told that this term we were to learn water-colour drawing I cheered the occasion up by bursting into passionate and inexplicable tears.

When, in the slow grinding of the mill of years I found myself with a little girl of my own, I swore that whatever other mistakes I might make in my parental ignorance, I would at least see to it that my girl, my best-beloved, should learn as many as possible of the necessary lessons to equip her for the life-road through the use of *all* her senses, and not through one alone, as had been the fashion in my youth . . . when children were talked to day in, day out, and discouraged from using eyes, hands or tongue because these organs inconvenienced their elders. I saw my little maid playing a game by herself one wet day. She had found several motor veils, gaudy ones, and she was crumpling herself up in a succession of small heaps on the floor and slowly rising out of each in turn, resplendent in a different veil. When, much intrigued, I asked what it was all about, I learned she was " crocuses growing up." So next year she had a garden of her own as elsewhere told.

To come to the title of this chapter (and quite time too, you gossip) . . . the request one day for a camera of her own drove my mind on to the train of thought here so lengthily laid out. In the path of this new adventure, should I grant her request, I could plainly see would lie many a sugar-coated pill of learning, so I pursued a wily way to the goal of desire—considering, debating, hesitating, till her ardour was warm and very wide-awake; and then, but not till then, we acquired a guinea camera together, and I made it teach her all I possibly could. The little creature learned to judge light, to observe primarily the position of herself to the sun, quite a new and unsuspected amusement, then to grade the difference between full sunlight and its lesser cloud-modified degrees. As she progressed she drew near to a sense of proportion in seeing her sitters on the finder, and in touching the fringe of that sense she glimpsed the whole meaning of Art.

In due course the long wait between her click of the shutter and the shopkeeper's delivery of prints took toll of her patience, much to my joy; and so we considered together and ultimately got a daylight developing outfit, diving thus deeper and deeper into the meaning of photography. We discussed the action of light on the films, and gathered in so doing a wholesome respect for its power and activity, learning, by the way, that light denied to flowers and humans leads to horrible results on their colour and constitutions. We saw the unpleasant stains attendant on untidy or careless developing, and made a solemn rule never by any chance broken, that everyone should leave the camera room spotless after use; dishes, tank, apron, box—everything washed, dried and put away. An exercise in orderly habits!

The passage of years has confirmed me in my idea that a child's camera is a valuable aid to education, along paths so pleasant that interest is stirred afresh at every turn, and the rust and mildew of the soul, which are the legacy of boredom, never get a chance to appear. Now that the mechanical part of her hobby is well mastered, the child begins to show individuality. The portrait here given was evolved in the days when she had to acquire a sense of proportion and of perspective; had it been an

"The portrait." *Chap. II.*

"Her picture of the wood and hammocks." *Chap. II.*

NEW SCHOOL-BOOKS

effort of to-day I should have been inclined to class it as a well-defined caricature. Her picture of the wood and hammocks was pleasantly composed, we told each other, and many of her little pictures came to betray that quality.

Pursuing that same matter of the educational use of pastime and hobbies in forming life habits and tendencies in our little folk, I have long entertained a notion that more than a little of wholesome training was to be obtained, keen-edged with interest, in the care of pet animals.

Most children love animals, and, in education, I have passionately pursued an unorthodox idea, which is, that if people are very fond of anything, there is probably some good in it, so it is politic to let them have it and see they get the best out of it.

To explain by means of an example: As a child I was devoted to young things—a nestful of little birds, a cat with kittens, a puppy—anything like that would make my heart swell, almost to pain with its pleasure. We were not allowed to keep animals. In our penurious and well-populated household, I can plainly see that pets would have added an intolerable burden to an overloaded mother's work.

There was, however, one radiant affair which gave me a nursling for a while. One day, at prayers, peering between my fingers, as was my wont, I was electrified to see a brilliant eye regarding me while its owner sat and washed a whiskered face. I kept more still than ever before and was sorry when the drone of father's voice ceased and the upheaval of many kneeling frames caused the mouse to scamper home. I noted its hole and furtively baited my prayer spot with trifles of bread saved from breakfast every day as soon as I kneeled down. The little mouse became very tame. I believe it truly got to know me, for it often came and sat quite close to my chair-leg, and I yearned in a sort of agony to touch its soft brown fur and feel its scraping feet on my hand. But that would have betrayed me to the devout paternal eye and finished the happy secret. It was enough of intrigue successfully to drop a few crumbs near the wainscoting as I turned me around to kneel.

At the first general scrape of chairs, the mouse would come up and feast; at the second, which meant we were rising, with a flicker it would vanish home. I loved him very dearly, and his presence brightened beyond belief that daily boredom of prayer-time in my tale of days. But one unlucky hour a small brother inclined his chair to an unwonted angle and spied the treasure. A scandalous squeal of joy drowned the morning ritual. "Maywee has a mouse!"—and goodness knows how bitterly I hated my little brother in that moment.

The crumbs were seen, I was denounced for encouraging vermin, and a mouse-trap enlisted—to my inextinguishable horror.

Thinking over the affair of my poor little mouse in after years, I felt sure that brief experience as tamer and lover of live stock had been good for me, short as it was. Analysing my emotions I realised that they had been protective and kindly towards the small creature, and I opined that in such impulses lie the seed of parental love and good citizenship. I reflected that these budding qualities might be trained to robust growth, if guided and directed from their inception. Whenever I have an idea, I want to work it out at once; I am not good at waiting. . . .

So I no sooner heard my small child admire a kitten one day than—regardful of theories—I set forth to get her a pet. It was a dormouse in a little cage, where he had a wheel to exercise upon. She sat on my knee while I explained the daily need of food and cleanliness, and we gave it a meal forthwith—whereat much mutual content. But when she was alone with it, she experimented in some way with the treadmill affair in the centre of the cage and crushed the little chap to death.

Her complete lack of emotion at this event so shocked me that I realised I was starting much too young, and we gave pets a rest till about four years later, when we had climbed to the peak of hearts' desire and lived in a garden and a real cottage in the country, instead of a flat in town.

A kindly peasant brought " the young miss " a baby rabbit one day for a pet, and my ancient theories awoke again to renewed life. We built a suitable hutch for the rabbit, named it, learned its needs and tastes, and after careful and prolonged supervision of a daily routine in the correct care of her dependent, I left the young woman to take entire care of her charge. For a while all was well; she sallied forth with the necessary equipment for toilet and domestic cleansings each morning and displayed some enthusiasm in begging greenstuff, or collecting it from hedge and woodland, to provide a varied menu. I lay back in the arm-chair of self-congratulation and mused upon the pleasant paths along which my well-beloved was learning her life-lessons.

But again I was wrong. The little girl acquired a battledore and shuttlecock, and, in the thrills of this new enticement, forgot her rabbit; and when it threatened to die of starvation, I took it away from her and decided I was a theorising fool, or else that my progeny was so modern that it contained no well-spring of maternal love at all. I discarded the idea of pets and concentrated on other ways of training.

But, long after, when she was sixteen indeed, the complexion of matters changed. She suddenly collected a tabby kitten of her own called "Dipper," and became a prey to the most violent maternal cares. The tiny thing was unable to lap when she got it, was hardly able to disgorge a mew from its small frame, and was an out-and-out mongrel. Perhaps the contrast between this helpless derelict and the fat, well-cared-for Siamese thoroughbreds which infested the home awoke some deep source of pity. Anyhow, whatever touched the mainspring of her tenderness, I suddenly found myself sharing the house with quite a new person, with a tender-browed Madonna face, unknown to me before—something I had dreamed of in my own far-off still hours of creation, but had almost forgotten to hope for in the self-willed youngster whom I had, so far, learned for mine.

I walked with my soul on tip-toe, watching this new thing. The wee cat was combed daily; it was fed five times a day—strictly to time I noticed—on fresh goat's milk out of an eye-dropper; it was put to bed on the stroke of the clock; and all this patient sensible care was given voluntarily with never a word of advice or praise from me. It seemed to well, like mother-love, from some deep, persistent source.

The small "Dipper" flourished exceedingly and the fevered attentions of "Mamma" steadied into a daily routine of affectionate supervision, which was all he now needed, and told me for certain that modern though she might be—and thoughtless as she had once been—whether by Nature's own doing or by some reflex of her early and discredited training, my lassie was true woman ; and an added joy had come to blossom in the days because of her.

CHAPTER III

PERSONALITIES IN A GARDEN

> . . . Need we care,
>   What is to come?
> . . . We have fulfilled ourselves, and we can dare
> And we can conquer, though we may not share
>   In the rich quiet of the afterglow. . . .
>   W. E. HENLEY.

AGAINST the background of country life personalities stand out with lively clearness; the possession of a garden and a number of friends is almost like having a private cinema of one's own! When I focus this Surrey garden through the perspective of years it shows itself to have been a frame for many pictures; portrait after portrait swims into view, of people known slightly in the artificial light of social life in London who have come as guests to the cottage blissfully unconscious of the piercing ray in which their true selves will speedily stand discovered.

For no one can pose or do Society stunts in the garden of a true gardener. The skins of affectation are speedily sloughed, the tension of a myriad efforts to keep pace with life in London relaxes in the simple order of our unostentatious days, and presently the dizzy guest-feet cease trying to dance their mad measures, seeing that none are watching or wanting their efforts to please. They learn to rest among the flowers. I know the process so well: the jaded faces renew their youth; the forced wit, corseted with epigram, dies away into spontaneous silences, and then the fun begins. For as each one loses the acquired, artificial self the submerged real human being creeps out, wavering and weak at first as a butterfly from its cocoon.

Filmed by memory upon the screen of the garden I see many merry actors pass, expressing with violence and all unconsciously their hidden tastes; or, with unknowing pathos, their lost desires, their distant hopes. I am trying to express—but lamely, I know—a very real side to my garden life, one that only experience has unfolded through the years, and that I but dimly sensed in the days of first ignorance. I was dazzled with joy then, as a new married bride and groom in the glamour of their honeymoon. After long years of companionship I am learning the secret sweetness of her quality, and one I dearly value is this power in the soul of my garden to press from the harassed, hurried, city bruised hearts of my friends the restful beauty of themselves at rest.

My garden once unmasked a volcano. Many strange characters passed beneath its clear ray

PERSONALITIES IN A GARDEN

during the four long years of war, but truly the Californian was the most astonishing. Before the gigantic struggle in which gasping Europe swayed wore to a close, there came to our Island ears a mighty rushing sound of millions of men new dedicate to arms; and presently they began to arrive on our shores—magnificent stalwarts, sons of that young race which is our firstborn child—our high-spirited adventuring child which we lost, and have but now cause to hope we may find again, grown to man's estate and pride.

The young Crusaders filled our towns—drifting through the storied countryside, observant and remote—with goodness knows what of unvoiced criticism and comment, though here and there a voice, clear and ringing, would shape itself into words among his people of what he saw; and we, a nation breathless, dizzy, at death-grips—would feel rather than hear the trumpet call of young wonder in our midst. Of such was Merrill.

There was a phase of this invasion of our island by our American allies when we were officially asked to show something of English home life and kindness to lonely Americans. In my passionate obedience to every request of a national kind I imported a stalwart, therefore,—who commenced every conversation with " In the West where I come from——," telling tales of his home as if he hailed from an unknown land. In time, finding most of the company knew America and had lived or visited there, or had some blood connection with its natives, he lapsed into observant silence, from thence to a keen interest in the daily round, and, lastly, into a devouring activity.

It was the honey started it. By dint of long search and some poultice of backsheesh craftily applied to a peasants' aching palm, the daughter of the house secured four sections of clover honey in the comb. It appeared, refreshing as rain in a drought, upon the jamless, sugarless, war-breakfast table, to the extreme delight of the Californian. Like most Americans, he refused all alcohol in the form of beer, spirits or wine, preferring his system to manufacture its own by supplying it with large quantities of sugar; and the shortage of "candy" hit hard at his comfort. I sympathised abundantly with his flattering devotion to the breakfast table after this reinforcement of its menu, and promised him that when next he came down on leave, any harvest of heather honey which we could get from the hives should be reserved for him alone.

This prospect served to sharpen his interest in bees to a desperate point. With the thoroughness and energy of his race he proceeded to steep himself in bee-lore; every textbook on agriculture, from Cowan to the romantic Maeterlinck and Tickner Edwards, was devoured and apparently digested, for presently I became aware of an uneasy spirit at

"The American passed across the garden-life like a cyclone, leaving behind him splendid new hives." *Chap. III.*

my board. "Weren't my bees Dutch bees?" I said they were. "Did I know Dutch bees were given to swarming fever?" I did. "Had I any spare hives?" I confessed I had not. Pressed for reasons I explained that, in common with most beekeepers, I was endeavouring to evade the ravages of Isle of Wight Disease by breeding only Dutch or Italian bees; that I had scoured the country in my scanty leisure for spare hives, but that wood and labour being scarce, it seemed we must go without, and chance losing swarms if we could not sell or "unite" them.

The lone American, the loose-limbed, the broad-shouldered, the keen-eyed, thereupon announced his intention of making some hives himself. And from that moment the place ceased to be mine in any shape or form. In every room one found tools, *chests* of tools, rows of steel jack-planes, bit, brace, bench, vice, Stanley dovetail tongue and groove plane, rip saw, fret saw, cross saw, mitre saw, key saw, hack saw, every kind of saw, punches neatly arrayed in round cases, chisels of razor sharpness, nails in greater abundance and size than ever I had dreamed that nails could aspire to, sandpaper, emery paper, pinchers, clippers, T-squares, grindstones—all these and many, many more that I can name heralded the eruption of his volcanic assistance; he collected a varied assortment of wood, mostly rough and much very green, from all over the place, bringing instalments back on cabs or his back, whichever was handiest.

And then the clatter began. From earliest dawn till the last flicker of daylight the cottage reverberated to the echo of his toil. The study, the parlour, and at last the lawn filled up with shavings and astonishing language—Ye Gods, how profane a busy American can be!—for the wood, being of the roughest, needed hard planing. Signs of an early swarm in the busiest hive galvanised him into demoniacal exertions: the chorus of plane, saw and hammer ascended ceaselessly from this placid house.

One might as well have tried to cage Niagara in a bucket as stem the torrent of that man's devastating energy. He passed across the stage of the garden life like a cyclone, leaving four splendid new hives, two of which were peopled in due course by lively swarms, before he passed from our grateful hearts and quivering ears to the bloody maw of France.

You never know when you will press the button of a fellow-creature's mind to set the whole personality ringing. It never seems to happen in London—where most ideas, come to think of it, are exchanged over food, be it afternoon tea, lunch, dinner, ballroom, supper or Downing Street breakfast. But in my garden of happy toil and experience the effect of small courtesy or careless word is often paralysing. The debut of a section of honey turned my American soldier into a passionate carpenter; a tossed camisole turned an editor into a sempstress; a few words of desire for a sundial and a terrace turned a sailor of high degree into a stonemason, as set forth in the *Garden of Ignorance;* a few days' companionship with Tatty Bogle made the lion of the season of 1913 into a cat breeder. I will tell the story at some length in a cat-and-garden chapter presently, but the camisole affair was not so involved.

A very tall and stately lady, the best judge of bulldogs in the North Country, a famous horsewoman and beauty, was on a visit, resting before attacking the Christmas number of the weekly sporting paper she edits. The Only-Woman-in-the-World was indulging herself by way of recreation with a pet vice, which was sewing "cammies." All over the world living breathing creatures, from worms to women, are spinning threads which presently others will take and dye, and yet again others will take and weave on looms to make meshes, webs, drapings, fabrics, linens for hanging upon the patient limbs of the human race. All over the world little new limbs shamelessly bare are coming hourly into this sparkling globe; and the first act of it they feel is to have fabrics festooned upon them. Since this draping business starts so young and involves such world-wide industry it must have a prime place in life and deserves some earnest thought.

And that is just exactly what most people, both men and women, do not trouble to give to their clothes. They permit tailors and dressmakers to think for them, and to dictate to them, with the inevitable result that they lose the fine essence of raiment and fail to radiate that indescribable charm which personality in dress bestows.

The dictionary says: " A ribbon is a narrow strip of anything " . . . dismissing a vast and romantic subject, for, when we consider this matter of ribbons that definition is a miracle of accuracy, a miracle of evasion.

I know a little rock plant which creeps over the stones in the sunlight; slowly year by year, clothing them with a gentle grey-green—a uniform and very retiring colour, entirely insignificant.

When one happens to bend down and look close one may see that the plant is a fabric of beauty, made of myriads of tiny grey-green rosettes, stiff tiny cactus-like rosettes ; and, as though that were not enough in decorative effect, every rosette is spun across from point to tiny point with pale gossamer silk like a spider's web . . . I sometimes make people pause in their casual survey of the rock garden to bend and look at those pearly webs sparkling there. . . .

Let us do that now with this seeming dull and monotonous " strip of anything."

Come to think of it, ribbons are with us in all

the great moments of life ; the memoried moments, of hours that burned the brain; moments of birth, of death ; of happiness ; of duty, of grief, of pain, of gain ;—the moments which are spots of brilliant colour in the void of things forgot ; the moments poised in memory, hung in the abyss of things done and undone ... through all these beads of life threads the sentiment of ribbon— strong, unseen.

From the hour of birth we encounter it. Hardly a mother there is who does not contrive to bespangle her babe with ribbons ; many a pink-faced blinking scrap-of-delight I have tied with white sarsenet ribbon into its woolly bonnet and woolly jacket, woolly mittens, and woolly socks ! Many a mother-to-be, in old nursing days, have I attended, who has taken me on arrival to see the yet-empty nursery ; looking anxiously upon me with those meek mother-eyes where fear of death and hope of happiness clamour together ; and never a basinette or baby-basket have I seen yet that did not take the eye with fresh pale ribbon among the muslin frills.

In the hour of loss we have used ribbon ... found a moment's solace in it ... I do not mean in bought wreaths, those formal expressions of modern woe, but most of us have, I suspect, turned from looking upon our beloved dead to find a sheaf of the flowers he loved the best, and in tying them together, even in tying our sad little message upon them, have found a moment's ease from the ache of knowing we can do no more for him, for ever and ever to prove our love.

At the marriage hour what bride is there but hides about her somewhere a true lover's knot . . . a favour of white or silver ribbon which is really, did she but know it, the strand of a noose wherewith the gay groom she steps towards, so gallantly, shall presently hang her freedom. She is making the error, so common in life, of confounding the state of love with the estate of matrimony. Love is precipitation—marriage is evaporation.

It runs everywhere—the significant thread of ribbon that strings the sentiment of pathetic human folk. At elections, at race-meetings, the ribbons flaunt the preference of their wearers. Singers sing of it: " He promised to buy me a bunch of blue ribbons to tie in my bonny brown hair," and truculently, " Where is the ribbon I gave you for the sake of Auld Lang Syne ? " At balls—at dances, at carnivals, the air is spun thick with floating ribbons of paper, frail filaments of merriment, joyous and untidy as laughter itself. Some favoured few in our England may wear the blue ribbon of the High Order of the Garter. In the mad March month everyone who claims a streak of the Celt wears the green ribbon of Ireland; most of us have seen the recruiting sergeant, magnificent in

PERSONALITIES IN A GARDEN

eloquence, floating his favours of red, white and blue.

There is another ribbon that I wot well of . . . a magic wide and wonderful ribbon that unrolls before us daily; new set in happening; new garnished by the sky: the ribbon of the road, that unwinds beneath our wheels as we run down the reeling miles. In moonlight and in sunlight, in twilight, sunset, dawn, that ribbon flutters for those who love the road. Over the hum of the smooth running engine comes the lapping of the wind, silken fold on silken fold beating against the face; before our eyes there runs that mysterious strip of whiteness; festooned over mountains, twined through valleys, looped across the moors, stretched from sea to sea . . . the romantic, ever-changing Ribbon of the Road.

All these ribbons there are and more, the world's significant story-tellers calling the tale of human stir and stress.

Then there are *ribbons* . . . the ribbons men wear on their coats. Frail, intrinsically valueless, dirty, often badly put on, the sign and seal of a man's greatness. There is nothing more modest or more eloquent. Therein is our modern heraldry—in strips of vari-coloured silks; an expert can pick up the significance of a new ribbon as a trained eye can read a coat of arms. They are the ribbons that matter. We can never hear too much of them, or honour enough the men who wear them.

We know one woman among our friends, a Morris dancer, whose underwear always arouses our ungrudging admiration. She makes it herself of fine lawn for summer wear, and heavy silk for winter—of the simplest cut—her ideal being the fewest possible seams. The silk she buttonhole-stitches round the edges, and the lawn is edged with a tiny real lace, generally a fine " filet " or Buckingham. Then on every garment she traces her initials in pencil with her own handwriting and embroiders them finely. To this refined austerity she will add no ribbon. " Painting the lily," she calls it and claims, very justly, that good taste asks no ornament beyond the fineness of her fabrics, the perfection of their cut, and the beauty of her handiwork.

" Why be unjust," she says, " to those sheeny webs ? Take a finely woven silk between your hands and consider how much of care and time and artistry have gone to its making : the silkworms have been kept in the necessary poise of temperature ; the hands that wove their silk have been guarded like jewels, lest a roughness in their delicate surface might mar the work ; the eyes that dyed it have been trained to the very flicker of a shade—it is not just to so much of labour to snatch it and wear it without intelligence and without joy."

The lass I love greatly admires this dress-conscience; and toils earnestly to live up to it; in which I encourage her rather meanly, being but a poor needlewoman myself. Working intently one day she dropped a finished " cammy " on the lawn, to the frantic joy of Dandy, who nipped it up to bury with his bones. Our editor friend saw the disaster and made after the excited desperado, depriving him of his loot before we even saw what was afoot. While examining the frail thing to see no damage was done she noticed the assortment of medallions, where a sly sense of humour had crept into the choice of subjects in " filet motifs."

Cursorily enough we showed her how the trick was done, never dreaming this great Diana of the Uplands would listen carefully to such slow talk; but behold the miracle. Ever after she bends her stately head to the needle and sews medallions with all the industry of a cloistered nun. I suspect her of getting the long, dull main seams sewn for her by others—but that is only a suspicion, and her affair, not mine.

A squealing little migrant through the cottage and garden life was the war-baby. A girl waylaid me, one day, away in the heather-grown hills, to weep her piteous tale. It appeared that a flying man had bespoken her attention, and her mistress had commented without reserve. It was an " unsavoury scandal " and she must leave her situation at once.

Facing the question fair and square, without dogma, who can truly say if we live after Death? Whether this aching, loving, brave spark of consciousness goes on from life to life, or whether it flickers out in the dark. *We do not know.* But we can make a bid for immortality, through the children. Perhaps what the priests call " soul " is personality, and the soulless people are the folk without personality, people who have never thought anything out for themselves. The mirrors; the parasites; the blotting-paper people. We took the girl to our garden home; while we faced the storm of controversy among relations and friends, wondering the while why the world has not made room for mothers . . . only for wives.

It was decided to give the crushed little personality of the mother-to-be a chance to expand and bloom in the tenderness of a home instead of in the desolate mercies of an infirmary or a charitable institution. And on Christmas Day she presented us with a handsome male child sucking weeny thumbs in a cradle. Never before had the household met in such vital converse. Picture us there by our peat fire. The daughter of the house brimful of unquestioning welcome to the babe. The art critic, philosopher, and greatest of great hearts—delicate of comment; a war bride who had been a hospital nurse full of hygienic suggestions; a spinster friend who lectured on war-food substitutes, sardonically

PERSONALITIES IN A GARDEN

smoking; with the young mother passing to and fro among us, fresh and rosy from her great adventure at the Gates of Death; picture us plucking dried heather leaf and lavender to pack in a fine linen case for the cradle mattress; picture us hemming, sewing, knitting his tiny boots; and think how more than ever before in our lives we kept real Christmas! Unto us a son was born!

Over our tender task we remodelled the world—visionaries perhaps we were—pioneers perhaps—or lone rebels like Manet who was rejected at the *salon* and is now in the Louvre. We tried to believe that the day will come when women will be given their real freedom, when not the having of children, but the having of unfit children will be penalised; when women will be held wholly responsible by the State for what they produce, and men will welcome the honour of paternity which now they lie to escape.

After eighteen months of lusty growth, and complete possession of all our household routine and peace a worthy couple in the mothers' own walk of life, thrifty, kind and lonely folk adopted our war-baby; and responsibility passed into other earnest hands. But in its controversial sojourn among us were crowded many hours of real happiness. Over the cradle of our man-child we had at any rate held the lamp of love of country. There was something to our hand which mattered indeed. In the days of terrible destruction of life, there was life put into our hands to guard and fit for man's new heritage—the heritage of freedom so many dear lives were passing hourly to win for him.

There was never any question but that he must be adopted; crushed under a sense of social lapse the girl-mother's one idea was to get rid of her baby and hide her "sin." Her panic-stricken, shameless desire for self-preservation at any cost to the child, gave us, one and all, a terrible glimpse into the ugly workings of our social civilisation, of conventional motherhood upon the young and ignorant. I am persuaded that very little of the rough edge of blame or criticism would have driven her to desertion or murder. She was the most terror-stricken hunted creature . . . and most of all she dreaded lest her mother should hear of her baby. Poor girl; and poor mother to have won such a hard tribute. Not all our kindness, not all our careful silences could earn her full trust. She always feared she would be "left in the lurch" with her baby. An attitude to her sacred mother-work which might fill a thinker's heart with grief for the mess men have made of the greatest work in the world. I suggested to her that she could sue the father for maintenance, and so assure at least the shadow of a paternity for the little fellow, whether the man paid his weekly dole or not. But she shrank from me sullenly.

" 'E'd say I was worse nor nothing—and 'e was only one of a lot. They tell any lie, men do. I couden face it."

Sadly enough I realised that what she said was often true. To-day . . . but too late for her, she has now given up her child . . . medical science has found a blood-test which establishes paternity. A discovery of limitless importance ; one that will do more than anything else, I truly believe, to further the freedom of women in the widest and most responsible sense.

. . . . .

They come and go from year to year, from time to time, these kaleidoscopic changing personalities ; but amid all their restless flow the garden abides, and, anchored to its constant beauty, my heart rides, observant and content, upon the tide.

CHAPTER IV

"AWE-TIME" AND THE BULBOUS HOUR

> Tears . . .
> Rise in the heart and gather to the eyes
> In looking on the happy autumn fields,
> And thinking of the days that are no more.
>
> TENNYSON.

I KNEW a sculptor who used to call the fall of the year the "Awe-Time" when he was a little boy. The word autumn meant nothing to him, but it sounded in his baby ears like "awe-time," which meant much, for he was one of those dedicated from birth to the sad gift of poetic understanding and a seer's long vision. The patter of dropping leaves, the whimper of stripped boughs, a little muttering of thin winds among dead bracken in the dawn—such small things as these smote on the chords of his heart with might; smote and made music in his life, which he interpreted, according to the measure of his gift, for his fellow-man.

And to me the word has become the real name of the fall of the year. For I know well the fear and beauty of the great death-in-life, the profound and perilous slumber which is about to overtake all that which dwells within the soil. I, too, am awed as the abounding, surging sap drops back to earth from trunk and stem and bough; as the careless leaves fall from their high places, stop dancing and become still; as the ominous mists come down to shroud our valley, and the midnight stars crackle in a frosty sky. In the old days of deep garden ignorance I was conscious of nothing but the enfolding sadness of the season, and yielded luxuriantly to it, as self-indulgent mourners are wont to do to grief.

But the " awe-time " has come to mean to me also the " hope-time "—for I know now, being a gardener, that I may not linger sentimentally upon the contemplation of picturesque decay, but must gird my loins and turn to good hard work, for this is also the planting time of the year. The decline of each summer must carry at its core the promise and hope of next.

It is curious what a lot of courage it takes to plant masses of one kind of shrubs for vistas. It sounds easy; but I have known many garden-designers, even those with imagination, who quake in their bones and contract " cold feet " at the mere mention of an avenue of hawthorn.

" Think of the winter! " they say. " Why not alternate them with some nice evergreen flowering shrubs; then you'd have something all the year round!" But in effect, of course, you have nothing.

A few isolated splashes of colour, half, or at the most three-quarters, of the year; and for the rest, in the dead months, some dark green leaves. Unkind and unworthy words are uttered about the exceeding hideousness of bare boughs in the winter, and the short season of bloom in flowering shrubs. Yet there is truly not a day, year in and year out, when they are not beautiful, for with very few exceptions, the shape of growth is in itself a decoration to a garden which has any effort at design.

That voluptuous beauty, the *Malus Floribundi*, for instance, in April and May a very abandon of reckless bloom, an eager overwhelming mass of pink, dainty as laughter and challenging as youth, which lives its petalled hours so generously that neither leaf nor branch can be spied under the mass of bloom —even *Malus Floribundi*, which gives us such a splendid hour that we might well be forgiven for growing it the whole year round for that fleeting moment alone—has another remoter, subtler beauty, which only the stripped hour of winter discloses in the lyric confusion of its psalmody of twigs. Equally, the hawthorns, lilacs and many another one could name. Though I have seen it only in dreams, and never actually in any garden that my feet have trod, I know very well what a glory might be made of a long spring avenue of guelder rose or hawthorn, both of which give a deep and satisfying autumn colour, as well as the harvest of May-time bloom.

If I had a lot of land to play with I would make a great spring garden in some pleasant spot with an immense flagged garden at the centre, every formal bed bejewelled with bulbs, growing through carpets of arabis and myosotis, and radiating from that circle great avenues, each a quarter of a mile long. One should be flanked with lilac in every shade and tone, from the glistening white of Marie-le-Graye, the cold blue of Persica, to the deep wine red of Louis Spathe; doubles and singles in every variety the heart could desire my lilac road should toss its plumes to heaven; another avenue should burn with the fires of pink and crimson May; another Malus; another Guelder rose; another Almond; Laburnum; Rhododendron; Syringa; Japonica. Each would blaze its own individual trail of beauty, and fill the young of the year with unnumbered scents.

To every real gardener awe-time is the golden garden time of bulb planting. To the uninitiate it seems a dreary affair. They are the Great Unhappy who do not know the place of dreams to which we who love our gardens remove ourselves in the fall time of the year. While they, in their deep ignorance, look only upon bags of oniony things with brown shiny skins, upon trowels and groping hands, smelly bonemeal, and arduous bent backs, we, who are priests and prophets, see visions of pure beauty and lay our uncanny little babes into arms of Mother Earth with tender understanding of their needs and faith in her bounteous heart to provide for them.

Funny little fellows, bulbs! Their small ivory bodies so clear and firm, tight swaddled in fine brown silk, still make me catch at my breath with wonder every year that I handle them, in spite of the thousands I have planted. Here is this little, little thing, small and silky, the pointed round of nothingness in my hand, in the spring it will come to sight again garbed in a raiment of soft grey-green and crowned gloriously with rose and white, transfigured into beauty.

There are some things I never get used to. One is the sight of an aeroplane in flight, and another a parcel of bulbs. Every fountain of imagination flows fresh with wonder every time I see either; I am aglow with a sort of brooding ecstasy at the glimpse of what they mean.

It follows, of course, that a nurseryman's shop window is a lodestar to which my eyes continually turn. I press my nose against the glass, studying names and prices in honest admiration and envy; and this I do with my whole heart year after year, though I know perfectly well that the crafty merchant sheltered within has laid out his display for bait, to entice the silver from my pocket into his. I know, also, that he has a dreadful weapon concealed within his armoury of beguilement, which he will shortly loose upon me if he has not done so already—a thing called a catalogue—than which I know no siren more persuasive. I welcome these catalogues at my table, as they descend upon me in their season, with a fearful joy; one half of me terror-stricken at the Great Push which the bombardment heralds, and which I know full well is certain to out-general and devastate my bank account—and the other half secretly glowing at the prospect of planning and ordering my bulb display for the spring to be.

This is the kind of thing that happens: "Irises," I say to myself, "I must have English and Spanish bulbs; there is such a wonderful collection of rhizomatous irises here that I must have the bulbous ones to carry on the anthem. Crocuses are my spring delight, and their pollen is food for the bees. Crocuses I must have; and tulips for bed and border. Never, never can I write a bulb order without giving a great deal of space to tulips; and hyacinths for the big earthenware bowls to light up and perfume the whole house early in the New Year. And daffodils . . . who can love the golden banners of the daffodils more than I? Every year I order a few dozen at least of these beloved bulbs . . . and lilies, tiger, Madonna, auratum ; each kind of lily that my soil will bear."

About here I pause and turn to the intoxication of the catalogues. Under the apple tree on the lawn and on the hill at the end of the flagged garden, also in sundry other nooks and corners, daffodils grow " wild " in the grass. I must refresh these, methinks, with some new sorts, so I baptize the clean order sheet with its first splash of ink . . . one dozen King Alfred, for the lawn ; one hundred minimus, for the rockery ; and two hundred of dear old Sir Watkin, to cheer up the odd corners. I linger over the order as I write it, dreaming of the tiny fluttering cups of minimus which will pool like molten gold in their sunny pocket on the rockery, of the glorious show King Alfred will make. I have waited seven years to be able to afford him. Last time I saw a catalogue he was seven shillings and sixpence a bulb, and when first I met him he was six guineas a bulb ; so I had to wait.

Sir Watkin will never fail me. Him I know well and dearly love : a robust and hearty musketeer always greeting me with the same jolly nod. As a matter of course I put down two hundred pheasant-eye narcissi ; they *belong !* They with their curly wax-white petals, golden hearts, and exquisite perfume are part of the garden, and may not be denied.

Away in the corner of the herbaceous border, which is mostly yellow and cream, I must have a large patch of Spanish Iris "Thunderbolt," the great bronze iris, so a hundred goes down to his name; and two hundred of Blue Beauty, and two hundred of King of the Blues and Whites, to glimmer pale and frail in the summer twilight.

To succeed these there must come, of course, the fat bulbs of the larger English Irises, and I put down two hundred of each of Dark Blue and Rosy Lavender.

The queer, flat corms of the crocuses fill my mind's eye next, with their silly little whiskery tops, like misplaced wigs. Of these I know just what I want, two hundred of each of white, gold, blue and purple; but an uneasy sensation begins to tickle at my ribs that they have gone up in price beyond belief, that I have already been rather lavish, and that the tulips and hyacinths are yet to come. So I reduce vigorously to fifty each of golden yellow (large bulbs) Bleu Celeste, the silver azure crocus in which my soul delights and which goes under the study window, King of the Whites and Purpureus Grandiflorus, a long handsome cup of rich deep purple, which always seems to attract the bees especially.

A row of wide shallow bowls made with a rich deep green glaze at the local pottery, filled with peat fibre, shell and charcoal await the contingent of plump hyacinth bulbs which are to shine like scented lamps in the darkness of winter, so down go one dozen each of Baroness Van Tuyl, snow-white; Count Andrassy, pale blue; Marie, dark violet-blue; Yellow Hammer, the favourite gold; Ornement Rose, pale flesh; and La Victoire, brilliant rose-crimson. And then, flushed and fearful, yet tingling like a drug fiend near an opium den I turn to tulips.

This year I want to try what I have never had yet, and that is a stream of bronze and gold and cream under the terrace wall. . . . I have had deep black crimson with brilliant scarlet and pink; I have had yellow and white; I have had a foaming carpet of white arabis with Cottage Maid tulips blushing adorably through; but I have never had the intense warmth of a bronze and golden river flowing under the grey stone wall. So, luxuriously, I turn to the bewitchments of Mr. Bide's catalogue.

"Moonlight" is a pale primrose May-flowering tulip, I find, with long elegant blooms, so down go a hundred, and in front of her I shall have "La Rêve," whose globular blooms of soft rose-orange with chamois glow I remember at the R. H. Show of last June. Two hundred will make a nice front edging to the scheme of colour; the terrace needs three hundred, but I must economise; among the "Moonlight" I shall mix "Bronze Queen" and "La Tristesse," which last is a difficult bulb to

"AWE-TIME" AND THE BULBOUS HOUR 77

get, and is sold only by the dozen, so I must try four dozen. She has a large silvery mauve flower, inside a pansy violet with a coppery glow; to intensify this scheme I will have a hundred " Ingelscombe Yellow," a pure and glossy canary gold; and two hundred each of the deep " Don Pedro," coffee brown and mahogany—and " La Tulipe Noire," which we all know for its large black bloom.

I have no idea how they will really turn out, massed under the grey wall; but that is the fun of it all, they sound wonderful. To have some tried and trusted friends to fall back on I put down two hundred each of " Clara Butt," the delicate rose tulip; " Couleur Cardinal "; " Gesneriana Major," to give me a distant blood crimson glow; and three hundred of our dainty old love, " Cottage Maid." She shines in rose and pink every year on rockery and border, generally with sentimental forget-me-nots languishing near or bridal effects of arabis. In ordinary years these things want replenishing only, but five years of arduous self-denial in garden luxury has made my borders a wilderness. This stock will last some time; I must not be mean this year of Victory and Peace; I flourish the pen and add a hundred each of " The Fawn," a wonder of rosy buff, and the " Zebra," a marbled loveliness of purple, lilac, grey and white—just for luck.

About this time in my adventure I begin to hunt up prices and mark them alongside the order.

A prickling sensation on the scalp tells me my hair is rising. In a perspiring fright I add up the total, it is £52 16s. 6d.

Anon I depart to bed with a cold bandage round my head.

CHAPTER V

THE HOOLIGAN AND THE PICNIC

... O for a breath of the sea ! ...
For . . . women . . . garbed not so differently from the men, joining with them in their games and sports, sharing also their labours ; free to grant or withhold their love, the same as the men ; —comrades together, equal in intelligence and adventure. . . .
EDWARD CARPENTER.

AFTER many years with dogs we were left without one, a house that loves them and finds itself without a dog is constantly aware of a gap somewhere in the family pattern ; of something missing that is part of the household.

One day I saw an advertisement in the *Morning Post*, offering a thoroughbred Yorkshire terrier to a good home. It sounded too good to be true, for we had long discussed how to get a game little Yorkshire to befriend the house and share our walks. So we wrote, offering our hands and hearts ; and in due course received a very charming letter from a naval officer's wife, saying frankly that the little dog bit her children, and so she had to part with him, but they all loved him very much and wanted to be sure he had a happy home—might she bring him to London and introduce him?

So one afternoon a pretty lady appeared with a silken mass of tan and silver bustling along at the end of a lead. A nancy fellow he looked in all his glossy frills and curls, and her tale of his true nature seemed almost incredible in view of his appearance.

"He's a hooligan," she said; "he fights other dogs, and bites babies. Can you stand him?"

I regarded the he-devil, sitting at her feet, looking like a cherub in all his gorgeous vestment of satiny shampoo and brush. From beneath his fringe the gleam of a saucy eye was the only evidence that his mistress spoke truly.

I told her I had no babies for him to bite, and that I was renowned for separating fighting dogs; and we thereupon made a bargain between one another: (1) that if he did not get on at home I would send him back to her; (2) that if we kept and grew fond of him that she would not ask for him back.

She bade him farewell with obvious regret, and as she went out of the door leaving me with her dreadful treasure, I seemed to see a picture of him being washed and brushed for the sacrifice, and his lady bending, just before she brought him in, to fluff his coat up anew, as people do in show-rings, with kind anxiety for the little chap to make a

"The cottage; deep-set in pine and bracken, where the Hooligan makes merry with bones." *Chap. I*

good impression and win himself a cosy pitch in life.

On the way home in the train that night, Dandy bit two people, and growled whenever I spoke to him. He hated his head to be touched, I noticed, and bit people when their feet came too near his face, which lay between his paws on the floor under a seat. He was fond of travelling and used to it, it seemed, for he understood trains at once and smuggled himself into the darkest corner without the least fuss. An idea occurred to me which I suggested to the family at dinner, and after it was over we pursued the matter by holding a consultation on his mouth. He struggled and cried, but was relieved of three very bad teeth without more ado, and a fourth we left as it was only beginning to decay, promising ourselves to pull it out directly he bit anyone again.

In a very few days his mouth was healed and sound, and the nervous irritability had quite left his temper, but his mistress had told the absolute truth about him, for he is an inveterate fighter and a hooligan all right. An entirely self-absorbed little dog, with a lot of personality and infinite courage ; almost, but not quite, indifferent to the humans about him, much busied with a complicated scheme of bone burying, about which business he displays a queer range of cunning, ability and industry, though I have never found out yet whether he is hoarding his bones against some unforeseen lean years or whether he ripens them like stiltons in the burial spots, and eats them in secret at epicurean leisure.

He nearly gave his life in defence of a bone one day when a hulking big coward of an Airdale came stalking down Dandy's own garden-path and tried to pinch his bone. The fight was a desperate one. I heard on arriving home at night ... to find, instead of the usual friendly tail wagging at the door, a faint and bloody heap lying in a basket. We thought he had gone, and were exceedingly unhappy, but he responded to judicious nursing, being a very healthy little chap, and in about ten days was beginning to limp around and hunt for more bones.

One night, about a week after his fight, he started crying in the most lamentable way. I hurried into moccassins and a wrapper and went downstairs to find half the household had risen to come to his assistance. It seemed he had been dreaming his fight all over again, and a horrid nightmare it appeared to have given him. We pulled out the last decayed tooth and gave him a dose of castor oil; he has never dreamed very much since.

The fearless spirit of the little wretch is always leading him into scrapes. He cannot bide at home to fawn and lick his way into favour, he must be up and out about some affair or another all the time; it did not take him more than a day to lose his beatific appearance, once we had taken possession of him. His lustrous clouds of silken hair trailed into wisps and bedragglements as soon as he found the heather and bracken in the wood, with the attractive big field of gorse over the way. He presented himself at the front door less than twenty-four hours after I had been presented with him in speckless splendour, a tousled wet and ragged tramp, with only one recognisable feature about him and that was the unquenchable gleam of his happy eyes.

We speedily realised that we had acquired no lap-dog, and let him gang his ain gait, liking him none the less for being independent, and only insisting on a few formalities of obedience for convenience sake.

He never really took us to his heart till his big fight, and after that he became our very own little dog, for he was grateful for careful nursing, and told us so in his casual way. We learned his habits, which were quite settled and reminded us of some of our friends. He behaves like a crusty old bachelor, getting up very cross and livery in the morning, and glaring about him morosely until he is given his morning tea ; after which he bustles to the garden gate to meet the butcher-boy, whom he adores. Then work starts in earnest ; we see a big red bone walking all over the wood and garden with an overweighted Dandy, very worried and important at the end of it. He turns up hours after having secreted the treasure somewhere, very muddy on the nose, to see who is going for a walk, and especially if any letter-writing is afoot, for that always means a scamper to the pillar-box at the top of the hill, where a pink-nosed Pekingese lies in wait to exchange chit-chat and snarls.

When the muzzling order was on he was very truculent, and persisted in wearing his muzzle on the back of his head like a bonnet, which upset us and made us argue with him, for these troublesome laws are made for some reason, and it is best for the general good that they should be obeyed. So on the muzzle used to go, every morning after his tea, and off would go Master Dandy to wriggle and roll it out of the way before the butcher-boy came. He succeeded so often that we had to have one especially made for him, and his horror was extreme when he had to meet his friend the morning it was first put on, with a cage between himself and his bone.

We left him in this tantalising plight to make sure the new muzzle was really safe. And Dandy disappeared. We scoured the lanes, advertised, sought him at the police station, but for three whole days he was gone, and then he was discovered late at night by a passer-by, faint with hunger and half strangled, hung up in a gorse bush a long way off, in a lonely place.

THE HOOLIGAN AND THE PICNIC

He lay in the arms of his rescuer, weak but triumphant; with a rascally beam in his brown eyes, defying us to muzzle him again. After that he had to live on a lead, and missed his freedom sorely, poor lad. We were quite as thankful as he was when the order was removed.

As far as Dandy is concerned cars are not on the road, and I believe he is an actor. For when one knocks him down he lies quite still, apparently dead, while we pick him up under the eyes of a weeping crowd and take him into the chemist, where a reviving draught is presented which he laps up barking for more, emerging shortly to laugh at the sympathising multitude outside.

Cars at the garden gate are quite another matter, they become things to ride in; he has certainly acquired somewhere a taste for travel, coupled with a belief that it is as well not to make his presence obtrusive in wheeled conveyances, for he sneaks into the smallest, darkest spot and lies perdu till the journey is well advanced, when he emerges to eye his company and sniff the air. He secured many pleasant outings this way, causing our friends much trouble to restore the stowaway until we learned to look for him before starting and nip these migrations in the bud.

One day we went for a picnic, and there we lost him entirely. Our happiest picnics are those accompanied by the Art Critic, who has a rare gift of companionship, and this picnic was special because we had not only him but also another literary man, brilliant in conversation, and matters looked well for a long lazy day under the sun with the precious added refreshment of rare and choice minds.

Some of the inveterate athletes refused to go in a car and set off early to walk to our rendezvous. Dandy, who smelt a walk, tried to follow them—but the car-party shut him up in the study with a view to giving him a ride. When we came to look for him an hour or two later the window was open and he was not there ; so we decided he had followed the others and went without him, spinning gloriously down the romantic Surrey roads, cool in pine and bracken, with the deep blue sky above.

When the walking contingent arrived hot and thirsty at " Thor's Altar," they confessed that they had loitered on the way and made up time by taking a bus to Churt, which brought them within reasonable distance of our chosen purple hill. We asked about Dandy, but nobody had seen him, and we proceeded to lay out lunch among the blossoming heather, saying he must have stayed at home after all ; we put away his bone to take home for his supper, and relaxed ourselves to the caress of a warm and honey-scented hour.

When the labours of luncheon were passed, we sat around, sun-soaked and lazy, to hear our literary

THE HOOLIGAN AND THE PICNIC

friend read poetry. He had put Tennyson in one pocket, Rupert Brooke in another, and sweetly, in his silver Celtic voice he read the old, old lines of *Locksley Hall*.

I dipt into the Future, far as human eye could see,
Saw the Vision of the world, and all the wonder that would be,
Saw the heavens fill with commerce, argosies of magic sails
Pilots of the purple twilight, dropping down with costly bales ;
Heard the heavens fill with shouting, and there rained a ghastly dew
From the nations' airy navies grappling in the central blue ;
Till the war-drum throbb'd no longer, and the battle-flags were furled
In the Parliament of man, the Federation of the world.
There the common sense of most shall hold a fretful realm in awe,
And the kindly earth shall slumber, lapt in universal law.
Yet I doubt not through the ages one increasing purpose runs
And the thoughts of men are widened with the process of the suns.
Not in vain the distance beacons. Forward, forward let us range,
Let the great world spin for ever down the ringing grooves of change. . . .

"I believe the poets of a Nation are its prophets," ventured the gardener-girl in the thoughtful silence that followed.

The reader turned to her with a glowing smile : " Aye ! There we have it. Old milk-and-water, sugar-and-sweetness Tennyson gives us something that focusses our eyes far from the individual agony of to-day on the world-betterment of to-morrow. Poets are truly a Nation's prophets and seers. The Jews knew that, and preserved their wonderful Song Book to spur and guide their race. We have taken it over as our Bible, and endeavoured to hear its wild Eastern music with our alien Occidental ears; we have benumbed its melody with ceaseless repetition, we have cankered it with custom and compulsion till its beauty mainly reaches us as a Sunday task intoned.

"So though there is in the Song Book of the Jews the finest poetry ever written, the greatest human scroll from Genesis to Revelations, the most inspiring verse ever marshalled under type, we need not blink the fact that—take them by and large, people eschew the Bible as literature, and turn to their own prophets and seers for tonic. Fitzgerald, Browning, Brooke, Shakespeare, Tennyson, Keats—and all the other noble names which go to make up the Bible of the English which is being written into anew every time a poet rises up among us. The Bible is never finished, it is the book of all humanity, the Book without end, writ by every people in every tongue spoken of man. The Bible is the ladder of song left by the noblest voices in every country to scale the heights of Heaven. Poets are prophets! Singers are seers! They look into the future with a long vision—shrewd as Time and fierce as the flood-tide; an untiring gaze they fix upon the ultimate, a prodigious scrutiny incredibly brave and patient and wise and tyrannical. There is only

THE HOOLIGAN AND THE PICNIC

one other eye in the world that looks like that—the Mother-eye upon its young."

We were still; each in his several way digesting these ardent words; especially did I revolve them, for my youth was begloomed and beset by nauseating doses of that very Bible which he now presented in such an unusual and glowing light. While I pondered I watched a dull brown sphere above a near patch of heather which surely seemed to have come closer since I noticed it first.

"A band puts five miles on to the marching power of a regiment," piped the lassie; "perhaps poetry helps them too."

"Does music do that?" said the Art Critic. "Does a military band win five solid, blistering, aching miles from crying muscle and dusty feet; then surely the fire of poetry must help."

The sailorman, bluff and practical, burst out at that:

"What! Poetry? Don't talk nonsense. What can poetry do? Fill the belly or shoe the feet? Will it pay for their equipment or tobacco, will it keep them dry in the wet, or wet their thirst in the dry? Poetry! Poetry for picnics. We want fighters!"

For a moment we were hurled to the abysm of the material, and lost the light of the sun; but here the brown sphere among the heather rose and displayed beneath it an eager sunburned face. A young

Canadian engineer came forward, shyly begging pardon for listening.

"I had a day out of camp and you all interested me so that I have lost my manners."

We welcomed him warmly, knowing very well the rough loneliness of exile for cultured minds from overseas in those great camps. He turned to the sailor:

"After all, sir, what is the use of your soldier clothed and fed, equipped to the teeth, smoking like an Atlantic liner if he is without enthusiasm? He is like a car without petrol. Like petrol without a spark?"

"Well, poetry don't make him fight," argued the sailor lamely, conscious that he was on the losing side now this new ally had arrived.

"I don't know," said the lad slowly. "It is fine words that inspire him to leave home and comfort for the boredom of discipline and misery of the camps. It is words like those, "The path of duty is the path to glory," which make him go over the top at the charge at last, through machine-gun fire."

"You're dead right, my lad," said the reader of Tennyson, much cheered. "The miracle which can turn a man's body to face what it loathes and revolts from, is the tiny flame of Godhead which we call imagination; and poets with their vision can light that tinder in a man. Good food, good clothes, good

THE HOOLIGAN AND THE PICNIC

equipment can sustain perhaps, and aid it. They will never light it."

The sailor stuck to his guns.

"There are thousands of brave men who have never read a line of the stuff," said he; "the only man who has learned to live is the man who has learned to let life go. Every decent man knows that life is a currency to be bartered at sight for honour."

The morris dancer was much interested at these stalwart words.

"Life and love are very much alike," she said. "The woman who has learned to love is the woman who has learned to let love go."

They had lately had a tiff; and I saw the Art Critic's brown eyes gleam at her.

"What is this life?" I asked to turn the subject away from more perilous matters.

"Life," said the reader. "Life is light and laughter. The gladness of the sun; life is to face disaster with strength, to strain muscles of body and mind. To fight, to love, to win. It is to learn the loveliness of midnight stars; to gather in the net of our senses the lively fish of happenings from the ocean of everyday. To look fear in the face; to drink deep at the well of friendship; to take failure and success, good report and ill with wide arms. To battle and breathe deep, and fight again. That is Life."

There was a long, long silence. Then the stranger among us drew a breath.

"I knew there were people like you in England. And I have stumbled out of camp right among what I longed for; it's like a fairy-story."

He read us "Safety" from Rupert Brooke with a quaint little sound of the West in his accent; and then in the sunset we bade him good-bye and good fortune. We took his address, and gave him ours, and he promised eagerly to see us before he sailed back to Canada.

We never saw him again.

Most of the party, replete and shameless, had lost taste for walking and were going to pack close in the car. I found myself tramping alone with the sailorman, who had a worthy desire to acquire by exertion a further appetite for supper.

Down we plunged mile on mile through ravines and avenues of pine and heather, all our way glamoured by a great gold moon rising swiftly out of the East, while sunset was still glorious in the West. After several thoughtful miles tramped amiably together my companion dropped a bald remark like a stone into our deep and placid silence.

"Funny that Nature never made a wheel, the nearest thing is the human foot; that has a segment of an idea of a wheel in it."

The statement did not exacerbate me into reply, but it started wide whirling circles of new

THE HOOLIGAN AND THE PICNIC

thought as it dropped through my ears into my mind.

Wheels! They had meant a lot in my life, having a gipsy passion for the road and for movement in any shape or form; a passion distinctly traceable I have always believed to my great-grandfather, a wild lad of birth in the West-country who wooed and wedded a handsome gipsy girl. Memory caught me in her toils and I remembered the first wheel I ever saw.

It had been a busy day, for first of all there was a great clatter in the household, because something crumpled appeared on a pillow, which, I was told, was a new brother. I suppose my manner did not lead the nurse to suspect that I liked him very much; I was hustled out of the bedroom before I had time to scandalise a well-meaning parent by any home truths.

I protested at being led away.

"He is noisy and very ugly," I said. The nurse was horrified.

"Not nearly so ugly as you are," she answered, and for all the shortness of my six years, the idea that I was as ugly as that caused me exceeding discomfort. I went into the nursery, seized a little sister, who was pretty, and cut off her eyelashes, with a view to levelling things up; after a painful interval the mutilated beauty and I were sent to visit grandpapa, who lived in the same village in a lovely house near a famous trout-stream.

The unfortunate old gentleman found us an hour later fatally skittish among his favourite flower-beds. He so lost command of his temper that he hit me, being the elder, with his crutch. It was my first blow, and the shame of it, even more than the smart, filled me with outrageous fury. I was hitting his legs in a paroxysm of blind rage and getting well smacked back, when I saw a man flying down the road. The hedge came between me and the man, so that I could only see his head and shoulders; but from the smoothness and quickness of his motion I was sure he was flying.

From my earliest conscious moment I had longed to fly; and my happiest, rarest, dearest dream o' nights, a dream that I could never command though I tried often enough with bribes to God in prayer-time, was the dream that I was flying. It was a pastime that seemed rarely far, because I was instructed that in order to fly one must needs be an angel; and to become an angel one must first be good and then die, two things I thought dowdy and impracticable.

Therefore in the very article of rage when I saw a man flying I stopped short, sniffling and panting, to watch his progress; smoother and quicker than anything I had ever seen before he passed down the road. Rage was swallowed up in joy; I ran hiccuping to a gap in the hedge to watch the miracle.

There was a man on top of a great big wheel,

THE HOOLIGAN AND THE PICNIC 97

with a little tiny wheel at the back, and a certain reasonable understanding assured me that he was not exactly flying, but so near it that it might almost be called flying. I saw there was some truth in what the elders had said about the impossibility of sustaining one's progress in the air without support on the earth, but the motion of this new gait was so swift, so swallow-like, so amiable, that the thing I wanted most in the wide world was to copy that man.

Back I ran tear-stained, and garrulous now with joy.

"He is nearly flying," I said; "he is nearly flying. When I grow up I shall do that."

Grandpapa replied, distastefully regarding me:

"You can never do that. When you grow up you will be a woman, and you will have to wear skirts. Women can't go on wheels."

Again there swept upon me rage; including now, not only the old man, and the new brother, but Fate, Providence, the whole universe and a special rage against my sex. At that age of six years old, and in that moment I heard that there were limitations in being female. I shouted, sobbing and dancing:

"I will not be a woman. I will be a man. I will wear trousers and I will go on a wheel."

If only someone had lifted me up and murmured a little of the wonder of being a woman! Hinted ever so slightly at the boundless horizon of power, responsibility and privilege in Motherhood . . . ever so tenderly turned my eyes upward from the muckrake of revolt . . . why do people withhold the sweetness of the vision of living from little ones, and cramp them in a fence of " can't " and " must not " . . . why do they stifle desire and kill imagination ?

When I look back on the scene, with its intense futile emotions, its violent and summary punishment, I can still feel the throbbing temper which shook me. I doubt if it is ever wise to let a passionate child chafe at the limitations of existence. I had a sensation of having been trapped, of having been caught in a narrow space ; I had, too, a feeling that I was so strong to do this thing, to ride on a wheel, that I would turn myself into a man somehow. I would pretend to be a man, would wear trousers, would cut my hair short ; would deceive man and God and everyone.

I lay awake many a vision-haunted night, planning how to become a boy, and when I whispered this secret scheme to any of the elders, I would shudder at the laughter which it raised.

For ten years or so I progressed with this passion only partially submerged. It flamed up hotly on a day when I saw a woman with a safety bicycle. I had seen men, of course, riding wheels of a different shape from the one I had noticed when I was little ;

THE HOOLIGAN AND THE PICNIC 99

but I found one day that some were made with a peculiar curve down the middle, that there was no crossbar, no question of trousers, and I heard that women were riding them. Then I knew I had got back on Fate!

Ridiculous and pathetic the picture of the girl-child nourishing her infantile spite at being crossed; and yet on my pedestal of obstinacy, hatred and revolt, I stood, had I only known it, for all my sex; for the very spirit of my generation; and the bicycle forbidden and beckoning stood for the freedom women were denied, and had been denied so long—so age-long.

In my wild, abundant, reckless youth somehow an elderly man got tangled; a fact that interested me slightly enough, in my green inexperience of dalliance. I was complete in ignorance, swaddled in the heinous "innocence" of the approved upbringing of my time, terribly alive, brimming with fires and intelligence to which I had not the key, a very bomb of disaster to beset the path of any parochial bachelor.

He suggested to me that I might like a birthday present, and I thrilled with courage. I said:

"Yes, I should very much. I should like to have a bicycle, and please may I have it secretly so that I may learn to ride it and 'surprise' mother and father." (Whom I secretly suspected would need much persuasion to allow me to have it.)

So then ensued a series of assignations when I repaired to a far part of the garden to meet my admirer with the beautiful machine, the sleek-limbed, smooth-running, and long-desired bicycle; during which I learned how to balance, and " nearly fly " in the circumscribed space which, in view of the need for secrecy, was all at my disposal.

I was beginning to make some progress, when father discovered the machine carefully hidden in the coach-house, and came indoors dramatically to say that if it belonged to any woman in his household whoever she might be, looking very sternly at me, he would sooner see her in her coffin than on this thing. I was ordered with many harsh descriptions of my conduct to return the gift to the giver; which I did with loud protestations of despair.

In the throes of his unwise and heady passion the unfortunate disgorged a heated proposal, and I promised to marry him if he would let me have a bicycle.

And there goes still a picture in the memory-albums of an empty, very old church; of a spectacled groom at the altar rails; of a hardy young thing brilliant with hope and ignorance, hardly touched of fear, entirely devoid of any knowledge of communal responsibility walking up the aisle in muddy shoes to pay her price for the wheels of freedom.

And since then how many wheels have I ridden in how many lands! Trains and motors all over the world, sulkies in Australia, rickshaws in Natal, ox-waggons in Rhodesia, democrats in Canada, and some day I will meet an aeroplane: will spin on tiny wheels along the hard earth, mount on wide wings into the upper airs, breast space and taste the ultimate ecstasy of flying.

For all those old tales were untrue. Women can ride bicycles. One does not need to die and become an angel to fly. The positive people are mischievous liars. No man will make me believe now that anything is impossible to man.

. . . . .

The home-gate appeared on the edge of the hill. The sailorman, scenting a well-earned supper, took off his hat and sighed a deep contented sigh. As he unlatched the fastening for me to pass through I uttered a remark.

"I think Nature's nearest effort at a wheel is the human brain."

Which left him sufficiently puzzled.

Arrived in we found no Dandy begging for a much-delayed bone, nor any sign of him. Days passed, he had utterly vanished; we enlisted sympathy from the police and enquired far and near, speculating vainly on what had happened.

After two weeks had gone by without a sign of our lost hooligan, we could not do more than hope he had found a nice home, or that his death had been a quick and easy one.

We missed his queer self-sufficient noisiness; the butcher boy was a daily torment to us; we hated the white Pekingese at the top of the hill; we wanted to hear the pattering busy little presence about our feet again; we longed to stand still, heart in mouth every time a car drove by on our walks lest he should really get run over this time. We missed the trouble he gave us; we missed the miserly affection he gave us—we mourned him sincerely.

A policeman came one day to say there was a lost dog at a country town police-station many miles away; could it be ours because the conductor of a bus reported that a couple of weeks before a dog had got out at Shottermill and seemed to have no one with him. Hope flamed up. I engaged a car at once and drove off to the town he mentioned, without telling anyone lest it should be another disappointment.

On the way I tried to figure things out. Dandy thought he was being kept from a walk on the picnic day, so probably he pushed open the study window and jumped out; he was clever enough to have followed the walking party without attracting their attention lest he should be shooed back. Perhaps he had watched them get on the bus and sneaked in, hiding in his accustomed style; and then missed them when they got out at Churt. Yes. It might be Dandy; I tried to believe the lost dog might be him.

When I got to the police station an inspector told me a terrier had been brought there three days ago by a lady who found him wandering; he had a collar, but the name-plate was torn off (that sounded so like Dandy), also he said he didn't care if no one claimed him, he wouldn't be destroyed, as he had "took to the little chap." Rills of warm hope began to trickle into my heart; everyone liked our tiresome dog.

"What colour is he?" I asked.

"Silver and tan," said the man—and all in a minute I knew the hooligan was found.

Presently I stood before a long line of empty kennels for lost dogs; large kennels with huge chains. Handcuffed to one of them was a very unkempt, thin, worn Dandy. He looked so tiny beside all the appurtenances of captivity, so bewildered by privation and suffering, so helpless in all the muddle he had got himself into, that tears smarted down my cheeks as I took him in my arms.

It was quite a week before he felt fit to have a real good fight again.

Every New Year a handsome calendar or card has arrived for him from his first mistress, adorned with a picture of a Yorkshire terrier and addressed to him personally with a loving message. To which he has always replied with a letter to the effect that pleasant though this new home may be, yet it is not a patch on hers, and he is still her devoted Dandy.

Decoyed by these flattering sentiments the kind lady came to call on him lately, and I fear was a bit hurt because it took him a good half-hour to remember her; much to our chagrin.

We are wondering if he will get a card next year, and also how tactfully he will reply.

CHAPTER VI

FLOWERS FAR OFF

I

It is better to travel hopefully than to arrive.
R. L. STEVENSON.

OF course, December is not the time to choose for seeing gardens. I am well aware of that. But all the same, I fancy the man who told me no one in America had any gardens, and no one in America wanted any, was unwarrantably chilling. I could not believe him entirely. He gave me a long and rather cross talking-to.

"Now, look here," he said, "you may be a gardener or you may not. You may have gardens in England, or you may not; but take my word for it, no one here wants to be bothered with them. First of all there is no room."

I jumped at that. "But," said I, "America is a large place."

He seemed annoyed. "I am talking of towns of course."

"Oh," I mused, "I was thinking of the country." He was unpacified. "There is no country here. Who wants a garden out in the middle West? The farmers are too busy making money to bother with gardens; and there is no long twilight over here. Men do not go home from work to have hours of light ahead of them, so where would they find time? Also, who is going to grow anything to have it all frozen to death in one of our hard winters, as so often happens here? No; there aren't any gardens in America."

I went forth from this dogmatic presence highly unconvinced. I felt sure he was judging a building by a brick; that he had grown to know some special locality or State where such conditions prevailed; and that he supposed that the whole country was the same.

A good many people, when I mentioned gardens, seemed to think them a superfluity; but one day I was at a dinner given to the poet playwright, Lord Dunsany, by the ladies' side of the National Arts Club, and there I found some enthusiastic gardeners who told me that the spiritual beauty of the work has just as great a power over these emotional materialists called Americans as it has over the practical poets called Britons—the only difference being that whereas in my own land it has soaked deep into the lives of the people (colouring the leisure of all from the highest to the lowest) in this young country it has only just begun to appeal.

These people are always in a hurry. They do not take root in a place and grow slowly out of it, and back into it, generation after generation, as the British do; they do not, generally speaking identify themselves with a place so that in time it acquires some of the glow of their own personality. They are restless, seeking people, and I suspect that generations of assimilation and fusion of all their divers racial elements will have to work upon them before they begin to blend themselves harmoniously with the land that feeds them.

No one could call the Middle West farming a sacrament. Of loving tilth there is none. It is a rape and a race—a gamble—a fevered patriarchy indeed. Sometimes I suspect that architecture takes the place of garden-making in the hearts of these incredible toilers—for that is what Americans are.

New York is a city of buildings beyond compare. London is a dust-heap to it. It is full of aspirations, dreams, and epics frozen into stone. Buildings so stately in their majesty of proportion and of simplicity that they take the breath away and leave one dumb. It is like reading a book of poems of the gods to walk down these avenues and meet these red sonnets, these melodies in stone—each one different, each perfect, serene, composed with so fine a thought.

One day I strolled into a place of gigantic marble pillars. I found I was in an immense cathedral with dim altars at far spots; human beings were moving in this vast space like ants, their busy feet and voices making only a gentle hum in the echoing solitudes. Away in some distant inner temple I heard a voice—one single voice—intoning a chant. The religious appearance of the place and the secular hurry of the human atoms in it, puzzled me. I asked a man in uniform what it was. He stared. "I am not a policeman," he said. I realised it was a naval uniform of high degree and made hurried amends by using Admiral Beatty's pretty phrase: "No; you are one of our Brothers of the Mist. Forgive me for bothering you." His face crinkled into a real sailorman's smile: "Ah! You are English. Pardon me! This place is the Pennsylvania Railway Station!"

I make no shame in confessing I was staggered. It was the last thing I had suspected it of being. The sailorman was rather flattered at my bewilderment, and showed me that the shrines and chapels and altars were bookstores, hair-dressing saloons, information bureaux, ticket offices, etc.—that the High Priest in the Inner Temple was the official who called out the arrival of each train in the waiting-room. And then when I murmured there were no trains he showed me that they were down underground. No smoke, no smell, no noise. A temple for travellers in a city of travellers. Truly the Americans put poetry into their architecture.

To revert to gardens. I am glad I can assure those fellow-enthusiasts among my readers who by now must be strung to deep concern lest the New World has no gardens, that I have learned they do exist. From East to West the gardens lie, and also, mark you, in the Middle West, as witness Gates Mills, not far from Cleveland, Ohio, and Grand Rapids, Michigan, which not only possess gardens, but each has at least one that has become famous in the garden literature of the country.

On the Atlantic coast Philadelphia, Nantucket Island, Swampscote, and Lennox Massachusetts, are all famous for garden lovers and their gardens, I find; and as to the Far West, why one scarcely needs telling of the gardens men make in the Pacific Coast climate. If they did not make them they would grow alone, Californians tell me.

Considering the size of America and its great population gardens are rare, though the movement toward them has undoubtedly begun, and when this people gets hold of an idea it is apt to take it up very suddenly, very thoroughly, and work it to death—like the temperance reform which has sidestepped into prohibition. I would hardly be surprised to find the United States legislating in a few more years to compel every householder to cultivate his backyard; in which habit of the country I fancy I can spy their weakness and our strength. The British go slow. They wait for things to grow—to evolve naturally and healthily out of environment and circumstance. The Americans compel. They force; they legislate. A near-sighted policy it seems to me; but then, I am British, and a gardener . . . so surely no judge.

Not only in America, bustling busy land of town-lovers, did I find there were gardens, but I am certain that in the turbulent heart of ocean lurks a wayward comrade too. Sailing the southern seas, meeting the great Trade Winds sweet and very strong, I learned that Neptune is a gardener like everybody nice I ever met. Great borders of white spray, like arabis, bloom on his fields of lapis; flowers of pink and amethyst nautilus, the "Portuguese Men o' War" blossom round his handsome rock gardens of Ascension Isle and St. Helena, with clouds about their brows. The fountains of his garden are the spouting whales we see at rare intervals, and his air-folk are the crowning joy. I was leaning over the rail one day, idly wishing I could turn into a man and become a sailor, when I saw some swallows dipping and rising over the water; their little white tummies shone and their dark wings spread wide. Presently I looked closer, wondering how they got there, so far from land, and how they fed, when they flopped in the water and I knew what they must be. They were little fish—flying. I went for'ard and watched our stem cutting the water while the flying fish rose before us. Some were big—with blue wings and glistening bodies like mackerel. Some had four wings; some were so long in the body and wing that they looked like dragon-flies; some were little fellows like the first I saw, and, they flew in flocks just like swallows. The birds of Neptune's garden are fish that fly.

In South Africa I became conscious of an unpleasant failing. I suffered from envy. Maybe any other English garden-lover might feel it too, and would not blame me; but the pity of it is I know I shall never be able to lose it again entirely, as long as I live.

However happy I am in my Surrey garden, however my homesick heart welcomed again the tender greys and greens of our inimitable isle, I suffer a pang from time to time as I remember how I have at last really seen things *grow!* When I recall the little geraniums, verbenas, asters, stocks, salvias, delphiniums, roses, lilies and countless other flowers which we proudly rear to adolescence and maturity here, and then look back on the abundant beauty of the same things in Africa, I feel that England is just sent to try us, and that it is small wonder Englishmen succeed as pioneers when they can find in Greater Britain overseas such suns and soil to work with.

I never knew that African gardens were beautiful. No one ever told me so. I never read any garden papers or articles about them. They were as great a surprise to me as the peculiar blue of her hills, and the clear, close solemnity of her stars at night. People in South Africa love their gardens. So much so that coming as I did from restless America, I felt as if I had indeed " come home " to an England beyond one's dreams—a rich and overflowing land whose people were not ashamed to put love and patience, craftsmanship and taste into their homes.

Many of the houses are built in the old Dutch style, and have influenced the general taste in architecture to a marked extent. And however one may deplore the undisciplined Boers of to-day, with their casual ways of farming, no one will deny that they originated from a country of high ideals and unquestioned taste in art. I can never cease to admire the beautiful old homesteads to be found all over South Africa, but perhaps more particularly in Cape Province. They make a perfect excuse for fruit and flowers, with soil and climate to urge as well.

It is a pity so many of the buildings have been neglected for generations; some of our leisured folk who now scour Great Britain for old Tudor or Jacobean cottages and houses might well go out there and buy the old Dutch farms. I wish I had a photograph of the exquisite design on a gable which one man of taste discovered ; he suspected that the exceeding plainness of his ancient white dwelling might hold secrets, and got his niggers to chip away at the gable very carefully. Year after year the old Boers had slammed on a coat of whitewash—there were two hundred years of it, and it had hardened like stone. He removed two cartloads of it, and there found the carved design perfectly preserved underneath.

There is treasure-trove for lovers of old houses all up and down that long-settled, much-tried land of great romance. Some of the ancient farm-houses have exceedingly beautiful pigeon-houses, and slave-bell towers of quaint design. When a man had miles of farm, as those early pioneers often had, he needed a loud summons to call his natives home ; hence those picturesque bell-towers to which the Dutch craftsmen had brought their skill and love of beauty.

I remember ploughing through long nursery rows in Surrey one muddy spring years ago, and selecting about a dozen expensive azalea plants, then in bloom ; I chose them craftily for a very fine colour scheme, and in the autumn my plants arrived, tagged just as I had chosen them, so that I knew where to plant each one. After months, therefore, of hope and care, not to mention certain money involved in the small transaction, my azaleas turned up in the garden, and made a small display which was, of course, to increase in splendour year by year. The following winter was a severe one, and the whole lot turned up frost-bitten toes and died. When I saw azaleas in the light of that memory as they grow in Natal I confess I noisily envied.

Here every year I zealously try to grow phlox on my dry sandy soil. Manure is scarce and dear, and the struggle is severe. However, I do manage to get a clump or two of a fine white, and a much-desired " Coquelicot." Here is a scrap from my travel diary which shows me how the Coquelicot struggle ground a gritty mark on the skin of my soul :

"Here as I write (it being February and therefore autumn), a huge bush of phlox, large as a large rhododendron, flaunts its perfumed blossom. I peer at it through the verandah railings. I am full of memory, of envy, of admiration. My own little scrubby plants are thousands of miles out of reach of my hands in a pine-set Surrey valley, yet I seem to see every twig on their meagre bodies. It would be inhuman not to envy this lordly plant sunning itself in a blaze of colour and scent. Truly it is a lovely phlox ! . . . The veldt is green around the bungalow; away in the incredibly clear light burns the deep blue of the African hills ; pepper trees and gums nod in a drowsy breeze ; verbenas of unimagined luxuriance carpet the ground, and great bushes of geraniums are massed in odd corners.

FLOWERS FAR OFF

This is only a military camp garden, and not of any special artistic value, but careless as it is, it serves to set my blood thrilling with dreams of what a garden I could make here, where things do really *grow!*"

In spite of their nasty habit of making people sneeze, a pastime to which I am hugely given on slight provocation, I rejoiced beyond telling in the waving miles of cosmos when they bloomed upon the veldt. They are like tall moon daisies and range from white through every shade of rose to deepest mauve, blushing gloriously under the ardent sun.

With a true instinct for beauty the streets of Pretoria have been planted with Jackaranda trees, handsome, upstanding, covered in their season with sweet-scented flowers like blue wistaria. The intense sapphire of the African sky seems to have settled under one's feet as the flowers fall and lie massed, keeping their colour to the last; and at times the open veldt, too, will ape the sky when miles of those blue irises are out that they call tulips.

The garden of the Country Club at Johannesburg is one to which I still wander in my dreams, and some of the wealthy people round about have painted rarely well in flower-pigments on the canvas of their grounds.

I felt the difficult heart of Australia for a second

through her flowers; she is a harsh land not very kind to new-comers, but one happy day I call to mind away in the Australian bush. I had been taken for a picnic, and was with friends; the hurt of strangers was lifted for a spell, and life urged sweetly through the hours; the romance of small things—secret, intimate, unexciting but delicious—pursued my senses and made music for memory.

There was the billy-can sitting on a fire of gum-boughs—eucalyptus gum—the queer smoke-smell of which must be as distinctive and appealing in the nostrils of an Australian as the smell of a peat fire is to your Scot. Meat fizzled juicily on hot stones, and my companions worked swiftly and neatly about their preparations as people well acquainted with primitive cookery. Presently the water boiled; tea was flung into it; and in due course our mugs were steaming with real " billy-tea." Meat, bread, with a basket of Mandarin oranges plucked from a friendly orchard and still warm with the sun, made our feast, sharp-set as it was with honest hunger and taken in the perfumed stillness of the bush.

We stretched ourselves then in the sunshine and talked of men and manners, while one lithe lass who had loved my wonder at the sprayed gold and spilled scent of the wattle, set out to pick me some flowers to take back to Sydney in memory of the day. " Mimosa they call it in England," I told her, "and I have only seen it growing in flower-women's baskets in the streets; very expensive and bald—with the down all brushed off the little golden balls." She wandered off, and we tried to express among ourselves our several thoughts. They their questing hospitality, so eager and desirous to please; I my gratitude for the poetry of the untrammelled moment.

"Your loyalty out here amazes me!" I said at last, courtesies being stilled. "It's awful—it's more English than England. You not only end everything with 'God Save the King,' but you start with it too. And you not only speak English, but you are absolutely and completely ignorant of every other tongue. After the mixed languages of Europe, the mixed races of America, the French-Canadian element of Quebec, and the violent Dutch faction of Africa, this great Australasia feels to me like a crystal pool where the hurtling, boiling clamour of Babel is stilled in the cool and blessed deeps of one common tongue."

They mused awhile. "I think I know why we are very loyal," said one at last. "The Old Country is so far away that we are able to idealise it. That is the reward of distance to all loving souls. It has come to colour our Nationhood—this worshipping of a far splendid Island, where our King lives and which we call 'home.' It's Australia with us first, of course—Australia is our country—but the other is our shrine and bourne of dreams." We dropped into silence again, the luxuriant silence of complete well-being.

"Tell me," said another at last, "what Australia looks like to you."

"Like a pastoral country," I said. "All downs and curves, pastures and rolling hills—very rich, very dear to the eye of home-seekers; but I confess the eternal evergreen of the bush wearies me: and not even green at that. The gums are blue-green, a grey-blue-green, and they cover the land like grass in a meadow. I miss colour in this country."

"But it's here!" said the first speaker. "Have you seen the flocks of parrots in the Blue Mountains? Or considered the prisoned colour in Queensland and Lightning Ridge, where the opals come from? Have you driven through miles of orange groves at bloom-time or at harvest? And you must surely have noticed the Cootamundra springing like fountains of silver and gold?"

A dark-eyed girl slid to the ground beside me, her arm full of flowers. "Now look at these," she laughed, "and tell me if Australia has no colour."

The wild flowers of that land are like no other in the world . . . so full of variety, of sweetness, and of intimate beauty. They do not catch the eye and the breath as the crimson masses of Knysna lilies do in the valleys of Cape Province, or the anemones in the Austrian Tyrol, or the bluebells in our own beloved beechwoods at home; but they are unusual and satisfying both in scent and form, and in exquisite tenderness of colour.

I found my lap full of bottle-brush flowers, fluffed like the tail of an angry cat, crimson and cream-tipped, honey sweet; and of white bells like glorified heath; of wattle in white and cream and gold—downy as a duckling's breast; and long sprays of tea-plant, as decorative as Japanese almond and far more dainty. Tiny flat silken rosettes in pearly rose and white clustered close to the brown stem, and below them were last year's seeds, like rich brown buttons of an exhausting size compared to the pale frail flowers. There was also a handful of tiny brown blooms which she called, I think, "Baronia," or "Veronia," at the sight of which every eye in the party took on that look of reverent sentiment which we in England accord to violets. And for the same reason I surmise, for the tiny unassuming flowers filled the air with a sweet and lingering fragrance.

I gathered the flowers in my arms, and told them of the Surrey garden away "home" in England; of lilac and lavender, rosemary and may—till the sun sank flaming behind the blue gums . . . and only its afterglow lit their thirsting, attentive eyes.

Some day I shall write a book about Pansy Patch at St. Andrew's in Canada, where a darling woman makes time go softly among flowers in the autumn of her days; a wonderful woman, who has drunk deep of life and been unafraid—who has mothered all sad things and rejoiced with all glad things; a woman who has spilled out her ardent heart in sweetness, and turned at the last to a garden for rest. Other people's gardens are never a bore to the real lover. There are some I have seen grow up into beauty through so many years that they seem part of my own life. Away in the Welsh hills, overlooking the Usk, is one of these; it seems only yesterday that a little fiery-hearted Celt, with a slow musical voice, came down to our Surrey sand-patch on his great racing car one sunny summer, long before the war; he was pleased with our tilth and flower-loving, and began to unfold among them to the extent of confessing that his sister was making a garden and would like a chat with me, he thought. The idea so stuck in his mind that the morning he left us I found myself tucked beside him in the snorting, sneering Vauxhall at our garden gate, which presently bounded away at his touch; and, tearing over the Cotswolds at eighty miles an hour, landed us in Monmouthshire for lunch.

And there I found his sister and her garden, and have loved them ever since; I have seen her paved paths grow, the old quarry turned into a promising rock garden, the vast walled kitchen garden learn its proper place, and seen the slow successful evolution of "my lady's walk" bordered with roses and crowned with a noble stone seat.

We found a bush of white lavender together one day, she and I. Set up among the folds of hill and dale around the Forest of Dean is the Dower House, where majestic copper and feather beeches stand royally upon the lawns; a great church, standing in that tiny village, like an eagle among sparrows, assembles its towered mass in all the garden views. There we found a glimmering scented bush, at once familiar and strange, which we set out to examine carefully. And it was a fine rounded bush of milk-white lavender. We took cuttings, each for our several gardens, admiring the pale mist of bloom, thronged with white butterflies, yielding its sweetness, virginal, unresisting, to the summer sun.

Sanctuary is its near neighbour, for the towered pile across the road is the "Cathedral of the Forest," of which the story runs that once a warden of the forest was pursued through the forest by outlaws; in his extremity he trusted to the tradition of the sanctity of life in a consecrated building, and fled to the Cathedral. But the pursuers were not to be baulked, and broke sanctuary. The warden, preferring death in any form than at the hands of his enemies, ran with his dog at his heels up the tall church tower and flung himself over. The dog followed his master, and pity built for them both a handsome tomb in the churchyard which is "*for ever Sanctuary.*"

We went over to look at it, after we had tucked bunches of white lavender in our belts, and found it crumbling a little with age, very mellow and kind under the westering sun. The unfortunate warden lies carved in stone, with hunting cap and horn complete, and his faithful hound at his feet. I wondered if "Sanctuary" would hold good to-day; and spent a moody hour picturing fugitives like Crippen perched up on the tomb, hungry and cramped, with menacing minions of justice watching all round to catch him when he fell off from fatigue; and away beyond that stern circle howling hordes of curious folk yelping for his blood.

My sympathy has a most unlucky habit of staying with the pursued, and I consider that tomb too exposed and too unspacious to be much use as sanctuary. But the name sounds good, and the white lavender grows beautifully near by.

It is in the Welsh garden near Caerleon, loved of King Arthur, that the nicest bird-bath in the world is to be found, the water-divining one of which I wrote in another chapter, and there that a bird-lover spent a melancholy hour telling me how he builds lovely little wooden houses for his birds, and puts them in seemly spots in the trees about the grounds for them to nest in, but that as soon as the birds begin to come and survey, the cats find the place and parade up and down below utterly discouraging intending tenants.

That Welsh garden dwells in my heart as a happy place, known to me, quite different from a dream garden in Perthshire, unpossessed by any sense of mine but seen and loved in dreams through the letters of the lady who lives in it. For years we have written to each other, written in dark moods and in gay, till we have come to know each other well, drawn by the common bond of flower love. I do not know how her garden looks, nor how does she herself. Every year a box of waxen Christmas roses comes down to Surrey, and we place them lovingly in bowls all over the house, feeling the touch of her whom our eyes have never seen; but whose warm Scotch heart we feel very near.

There is an Irish garden, too, which we only know by letters, but it is mostly visualised as a place of trouble, where anguished questions are plied for help and guidance. Away in France a thrifty housewife sends us now and again useful plants or seeds for the kitchen garden, which we gratefully plant and coddle; but they hate our grey island and never grow as we know she would like. There is a German who knows my garden, somewhere; or was one, for Captain Griffin, D.S.O., M.C. with bar, found *The Garden of Ignorance* in a " pill-box " in the Hindenburg Line in 1916! And I have wondered, times, what sort of a Hun sat and read that peaceful story of an English country home under the lively comments of English shell-fire.

I saw a perfect garden once—also in Wales. It left me engulfed in unspeakable gloom. Everything that money, taste, site and soil could compass were there; and I reflected dismally that as far as that man was concerned his garden life was practically over. There was nothing left to strive for; a most horrible state to be in, and I went back to my faulty imperfect little garden-plot full of gratitude for the great need it yet has of me. It is the need things, and people, have of us which makes us love them most.

There is a garden away in a lonely place on the Sussex downs; in it grows a tall apple tree which blooms at odd times, speaking richly to those who live under its shade. It is as though a wandering spirit throbbed through its branches and burst out in voice of bloom at seasons unknown to other trees, which have not so much love about them. There is a great sweet soul in that garden; a soul strong to lose, and to keep, which pulses so warm that even the world-hardened stranger, passing through, is sweetened and stayed by its absolution.

Of all the gardens I know that one is the most beautiful.

II

It is not yours, O Mother, to complain
. . . Though never more again you watch your baby sleep. . . .
R. L. STEVENSON.

The moment that every mother remembers had come to me. "Here it is," said a voice, and I turned, weak and eager, to look at that which, so long, so lovingly, I had been creating in the dark. The nurse went off and left me to brood in the intense dumb rapture of my holy hour. It was a very downy baby. All its head was thick with soft black hair, there was a faint bloom of it even over its face! And on its ears tiny dark tufts like Pan's horns. Nurse allayed my anxious mutterings, and soon, of course, the little creature shed all its first-born hair, and grew into a pink-and-white girl with very fair locks, like any other baby of our England; only that it certainly had more hair than most little girls.

"Little Miss Muffet" they called her because of her big bow of blue ribbon each side of a round earnest face; Nanny and I, whose peaceful task it was to adjust those bows, knew they were there for a sound reason. They kept in check masses of pale floss silk, stuff which caught our fingers and clung to the brushes and combs, straight and glistening as the silkworms' spun cocoon.

As she grew older and more active these long

persistent flying strands became an embarrassment to her play. (In the picture the little boy has his mouth full of peppermint rock . . . long since sucked away . . . and its owner a soldierly cadet!) Reluctantly I entered into counsel with Nanny, and that faithful domestic agreed with me that, however much we disliked braiding those wayward sheaves of gold, it would be doing the lassie a good turn in every way. So behold her plaited and serious in acceptance of the new order.

Somehow the braids meant a new era to me. My unwilling feet turned toward the path of years, and I saw my baby growing out of my arms. . . . Does every mother-woman meet that hour? . . . Those long thick plaits were so grown-up, and I missed burying my face in warm thickets of tumbled gold about her little neck.

The effect of plaiting appeared to be to make the maiden's hair grow thicker and thicker, heavier daily, and at last we took to rolling it up on each side, it seemed easier to carry that way, but the little head was burdened, and one day a visitor dropped one of those careless remarks that linger and take effect.

"Doesn't all that hair take the strength out of the child's brain?"

A silly speech; her brain was all right I knew, but the idea rattled in my mind like a marble in a bucket, till I asked a doctor-man friend if such

"Shorn of her plaits." *Chap. VII.*

"The peppermint rock long since sucked away, and its owner a soldierly cadet!" *Chap. VII.*

a coronet as hers might be weakening; and he, contemplating the massy " snails " each side of her serious face said :

" It looks a bit of a load, why not cut it off and let it grow when she is older and has to have it up ? "

So one memorable day we jogged off to London-town to visit our friend, the hairdresser, whose pride it had been for many years to singe and trim our locks. To him we disclosed our errand, and presently his astonished shears descended upon the cloth of gold. I watched the rich swathes fall before his mowing, hoping the doctor-man was right and her birthright would return to her in full strength when needed, but what was my surprise shortly to discover my progeny engulfed in tears! I had never remotely suspected the little one of vanity, and sustained a considerable shock; mentally deciding that if she had taken to preening herself upon her abundant hair it was a jolly good thing it was coming off. Enquiry proved that Nanny, in common with many worthies of her class, took occasion to flatter her charge, a hateful practice, and had drilled into the receptive little girl-mind the notion that it was exceptionally beautiful.

Again my mother-heart took an unwilling step down the path of years; here was weedstuff growing in the lovely garden of her mind and I had to turn me to a new duty in our comradeship. It was not long before the bygone glories of the shorn plaits were forgotten in the lightened comfort and coolness, not to mention a sudden cessation of tangles. Came a day when a tall Miss said:

"Mummy, I'd better grow my hair, all the flappers have it bobbed, and I want to grow mine to do up like yours."

So yet again, and even more unwillingly, I faced the racing years.

She grew her hair, and one day, when I was away, went and had it waved and her photograph taken, "for a surprise," and over that "surprise" I draw a veil; for it led to a long and earnest talk about the vulgarity of waving hair that, like hers, has its own straight beauty of thickness, length and sheen.

Such a satin fabric, such a straight-woven curtain did not need to be tortured into singed zigzags. "Waved" hair is the restless heraldry of sophistication, advertisement of unrepose, the resource of undistinguished minds. We discussed the ethics of waved hair in amicable discourse together, trying to consider it from every angle; and decided at length that it involved a horrid waste of time and is certainly very bad for the hair, besides being too common to be attractive. And to this unfashionable belief we stoutly cling.

The years have moved relentlessly along; and nowadays among the changing personalities that frequent the garden is a highly trained and comely gardener, who flits in and out among the pine trees, over the lawns, and among the borders; this is a much-loved friend, a very special one, who has changed more than any other since first she came to the garden. I look at her nimble fingers budding roses, striking cuttings, pruning vines, pricking out seedlings, and remember the dumpy paws that used to stroke my face among the flowers, the fat small feet that used to trot so diligently beside mine. . . . She has changed in the modelling hands of Time from a round little baby to a gardener-woman; and though I love my friend the gardener mate before all others, there are times when I miss my baby much. When I hear a tall and capable Miss recommending sulphates for the strawberry bed, memory does .a " switch-back," and shows me again the little one who complained to me that her flowers would not grow " because they knew she was little."

One of the things I mentioned in *The Garden of Ignorance* at some length, was the incredibly foolish way girl-children have been brought up to believe money descends upon them, like the gentle dew from heaven, out of the pockets of their male supporters; they have been brought up to turn to brothers, fathers, uncles, husbands, anything and everything masculine for money, and never to dream of doing anything so unladylike as to earn an income for themselves.

The sentiments of disagreement with this attitude which I voiced at the time my book was published, were not, even then, so revolutionary or so arresting as to arouse any clamour. Many people were beginning to feel the same way, but the idea was only in the germinating stage. The forcing-house of War has brought this crop, among many others, to sudden harvest. Women on every hand recognise the necessity and appreciate the advantages of being independent. What I, as an advanced woman, was bold enough to proclaim as an idea for parents to aim at, is now the accomplished fact of thousands of young girl lives. And a very good thing it is too.

In the millennial far-off days before 1914, I was sunning myself in lazy speculation as to the career my girl might decide on when the hour for choosing came. I hoped she would choose surgery or research work, but I struggled faithfully to avoid the parents' ghastly privilege of influencing its progeny in choice of a career.

Then the war came.

The thick cloud of battle settled down on Europe, and life changed its values in countless reckonings. The submarine menace dawned. One night I was nearly killed by an air-bomb. These affairs jolted the career matter into first place for consideration. Being holiday time I sought out my lassie, and we had a long walk in the woods.

"I don't want to be dowdy or depressful," said I, "but let's face things, old dear. Suppose there came a nippier bomb and you were left an untrained orphan? I should feel most unhappy about you wherever I got to!"

People who have a vast horde of children get used to astonishments, I suppose, by the time they reach middle-age; but I with this lone chick am constantly meeting violent surprise. I had basked in visions of surgery or research work, sometimes dallied with the notion of a literary or musical daughter; but the selection was so far!

"May I be a gardener?" Somehow I had never guessed that the penetrating sweetness of the life we had so long led together among the flowers must be making its mark upon the young, beloved mind. I sat dumb in complete amaze.

"I mean to train as a real gardener, you know; pass exams. and all that. I could not bear a life that meant living indoors and in towns." Still I listened, trying to adjust a myriad prejudices to this idea.

"And no one knows how much food will be wanted with these U-boats all over the place; at any rate it will be useful work; people must always eat, whatever happens to the world."

I do not know anything harder to resist than sound common sense. All she said was very true. I spent a long time hunting up the merits of various

Women's Horticultural Training Colleges, discarding those which make the training a kind of expensive social hobby. If she meant to make a business of gardening I was determined that she should have the best practical training I could find.

At last I discovered a college under the direction of two gentlewomen, where French and English market gardening were taught, also picking, packing, grading, marketing, as well as the preserving, bottling, and canning of fruits and vegetables; api-culture, greenhouse work and vineries were also in the course. The full training is two years, I found, in pursuance of enquiries and investigations.

"You'll come home a blooming expert," I grizzled; "and then you'll laugh to scorn all my little humble garden habits, and I shall feel out of date and old-fashioned and a bygone legend and all those dull things I have watched my elders become; I simply hate it!"

And of course the darling arms were round my neck, and all this prophetic common sense was drowned in a flood of loving nonsense.

I sometimes wonder why parents do not secure more craftsman's education for their children. It is impossible to avoid acquiring certain virtues of patience, observation and thoughtfulness in the most elementary horticultural training, and the specialised variety she undertook entails a solid and valuable education in many, many subjects outside digging and planting, which most people believe is the beginning and end of gardening, with a sideglance at the manure question which is supposed to be slightly indelicate and better avoided. The mass of technical detail, the necessary study of botany and chemistry, escapes them altogether.

I spent a week-end at her training college once, and came away actively envious of the merry girls. They were being more sensibly trained than ever girls were in my own youth; their bright, young questioning minds were alight with interest, their hands were learning to be useful and supple, the beginning of all mother-craft was in their daily round, and whether they know it now, or never realise it, the sweetness of wisdom learned at the knee of Mother Earth will influence and irradiate their whole lives.

CHAPTER VII

BEE-CRAFT

> Thought is a garden wide and old
> For airy creatures to explore,
> Where grow the great fantastic flowers
> With truth for honey at the core.
> There like a wild marauding bee
> Made desperate by hungry fears,
> From gorgeous IF to dark PERHAPS
> I blunder down the dusk of years.
>
> BLISS CARMEN.

I BELIEVE one of the greatest pleasures in the garden is the presence of the bees. They are queer little guests, self-intent, and fierce in self-protection; not ingratiating pets exactly, but something so vital and romantic that a garden without them is like a harp without a minstrel; or a marriage without love.

From the bee-village, which is what we call the colony of hives near the flagged garden below the lawn, a sparkling stream of singing foragers darts up into the sunlit blue all the tireless day, and a golden cloud of them humming their note of deep content rises about our feet as we tread the flower-fringed paths. These may seem small matters, but they mean the presence of happy little folk around all the time, and that creates its own radiance in other hearts. From earliest morn the bees companion the hours of garden work, streaming endlessly from the mouth of the hives in an arrowy flight of gold; leaping from the dusk of their hives hung with daffodil curtains of wax, into the burning challenge of space, over the valley and away to the purple moors: in the cool hour of gloaming back they come spinning in their thousands, weary, devoted bodies laden with sun-begotten nectar to store in a myriad vats.

The pleasure of entertaining bees in the garden has necessarily been shot with adventure, for they require a certain amount of attention, which entails courage, and not even that alone, for courage lined with experience is the only perfect cloak in which to approach the hives. I can feel again with intensity of recollection the arrival of the first colony. A wire came late in the day to say the bees had been despatched and would arrive at the station about dusk.

Having forgotten all the little I had ever learned, long years ago, of api-culture, I surmised they must be met and housed at once in their brand new hive, which stood, sparkling in glossy white paint, in its chosen spot, awaiting the arrival of its " first-class swarm of Dutch bees with young queen complete," as per invoice.

Collecting, therefore, an adventurous companion, I hied me down the scented summer lanes to the far-off station to meet the new guests of the garden. We found a porter conscientiously stalking the newly arrived box; and he hailed us with sullen relief.

"Sooner you touched 'em than me," he said. "Last box we 'ad 'ere come undone. I don't 'arf like bees."

Fortified by this news my ally took one end and I the other of the noisy box, and so turned homewards into the summer night. He made things pleasant by telling me a long tale of a picnic party to an Indian Temple when Princess Pat and the Duchess of Connaught had to be saved from a swarm of wild bees that suddenly arrived, till my imagination, never a restful companion, was as stirred up as the excited horde we were convoying home.

Arrived there, we held long conference as to the best way to house them. It was now the early fringe of a dark, cool night, and common sense wavered at the task. We discussed a dozen ways of tackling the job, but every one of them needed the ultimate act of the desperado who would lift the lid of the box. Every device ended up, or began with, that necessary act. I endeavoured to warm the cockles of the soldier-man's heart with certain crafty offerings, cakes and cider-cup to wit, gifts of the wildest generosity in June, 1918. Perhaps the orange juice and ice and soda in it subdued the intoxicating quality of the cider; anyway, he remained cynical about the habits of bees in relation to man.

We ended up by taking the dusty road once more and searching a remote bee-keeper, whom we awoke from very obvious slumber to discourse with us from a tiny rose-hung window. He promised to come along next day at sundown and teach us to hive " the critters, bless 'em." All bee understanders become bee-lovers, one finds; and meanwhile they were to be left in the shade in their box as they were. Which we were well pleased to hear.

In due course he arrived next day, and performed certain magic deeds with a bit of board and a white cloth; opening the swarm box most nonchalantly, and shaking the bees out of it on to the sheet he had spread in front of the hive. They fell with a gentle thud in a velvety golden mass, thousands of bees, each one of which on the way home last night had loomed in my imagination as a great armed menace. Little, dainty, busy, melodious things they looked, concerned with nothing but the fixed determination to follow wherever their queen should lead.

The heavy buzzing mass on the sheet had a queer appearance to me, somehow it looked adhesive; the bees did not get up and fly about, but seemed to cling together and move as by a common will, swaying to and fro; moving, but not dispersing.

"It is the hive-sense," said the bee-master; "they will keep up their queen whatever happens, wherever she goes. Look! The scouts are reckynoytering."

Two or three bees on the outskirts of the close-clung multitude were crawling tentatively along the sheet toward the inviting gloom of the hive entrance, where the wax we had already set in the frames must have smelt very inviting.

"Hullo, you girls—here is a splendid pitch we've found!" . . . or something to that effect must have been passed along; for suddenly the whole solid mass began to move upward to Eldorado. Among the first to enter was a star-shaped crowd, which the bee-master joyfully said was the queen-bee surrounded by satellites and attendants who moved with her, every head pointed toward her sacred body.

Slowly, methodically, but with inflexible determination the entire swarm followed her whom they loved, her in whose one frame lay hidden the whole future of the colony; and fascinated, we watched the working of this model devoted community.

In our sandy garden we have in May-time and June cloudy bowers of white and yellow broom; it grows so magnificently with us that I often think the most romantic time of beauty in my garden are the two or three weeks when every slope and bank is crowned with ethereal clouds of white and gold. To stand in the pine wood on a windy day and watch the soft white masses sway and toss against the valley background of dark sentinel pines, is like watching foam on an incoming tide ; an idea enriched by the surging sea-sound of the wind among the tree-tops . . . only this is flowery foam breaking in fragrance on a sea-that-never-was.

Many happy hours we spend in broom-time watching our bees break open the delicate blossoms, which wait in tremulous maiden patience for their visits. The bees come bustling along full of business, quite practical and industrious, but whatever sturdy matter-of-fact impulse is animating their sensible souls, to the flowers they come as very cupids ; for the bee hour is to them their marriage hour.

I should be guilty of a literary theft if I were to describe the effect of the bees on broom flowers, for it was Percy Izzard, in his *Countryman's Diary*, who first drew our attention to it, and gave us thereby many absorbed and happy hours. I will quote his words, which are musical, and offer him at the same time our thanks for teaching us a new wonder to observe :

" When bees abound the broom flowers are soon in disarray. The explosion which follows the pressure of the bee as it strives to reach the hidden pollen is complete, leaving the bloom agape with a protruding curl of stamens and sprinkled with the fertilising dust. The hive bee and humble bee almost alone are capable of doing this, and their visits to the broom flowers are interesting for two reasons. One is that the exceeding plenty of the pollen appears to induce an epicurean nicety among the bees. They visit and open flower after flower in the refulgent mass, taking only the cream of the contents of each and becoming yellowed with their labours. They leave the bulk cast about the flower as the sudden splitting of the keel and upward burst of the stamens may have scattered it. Then their visits are the signal to feasting for a varied multitude of lesser insects that are always at hand. No bee troubles about an open bloom, but the latter quickly becomes a public dining-place for these hungry loiterers."

Bees are the least exacting of creatures, but some few ceremonials truly there are if one is prepared to harbour them in any thrifty and considerate spirit. There is the affair of swarms, the rape of their honey-store, the wintering of the hives, and the spring cleaning. Our first swarm was a painful business. I was composing the day's war-menu of strange device, when I heard a sound like an aeroplane in flight. A shout from the three warriors swinging under the pines in hammocks told me it was a swarm, and I hurried out to share the fun and ask advice.

The sailorman, capable fellow, went off at once to get the bee-bellows and make a smoke of brown paper; the gunner, incited apparently by memories of the former affray, put a jug and glasses on the summer-house table, but the American soldier was full of beans. He had just finished making a hive for this very event, and he burned to see it inhabited.

"Say, listen here," said he; "if you will read instructions from the book and stand by with the garden spray I guess I can collect this little bunch."

The swarm settled very inconveniently on the trunk of a quince tree near the pool, and our tall Westerner set forth bare-armed to collect it, swarm box and white cloth complete. I got *The British Bee-keeper's Guide*, placed myself as far from the quince tree as a decent appearance of courage would permit, and began to read the lesson of the day.

"When bees swarm they are gorged with honey and thus not inclined to sting," I chanted from Master Cowan's able script, and furthermore:

"If they alight on the trunk or branch of a tree, brush them gently into the skep."

There were detailed pages of instruction, but these two I remember with starry certitude because the American believed them so implicitly. I saw his muscular arms go into the tree branches and his bare hands gently start to brush the clinging bees. In a few seconds a volley of strange Western oaths burst from the thicket of quince, and a cloud of infuriated bees rose and flew out.

"Spray, spray!" he shouted. I looked round weakly for help.

Patently in the throes of memory the soldier was clinking ice in a jug of cider-cup away in the summer-house; the sailorman was fending off the attack of one persistent bee with his smoke bellows. I filled the garden syringe with water and sprayed the angry bees for dear life till they decided their swarm picnic was threatened with rain and returned to cluster on the trunk of the tree with their queen.

It was a horrid morning; each time the swarm settled that persistent American tried again to "collect" it, till he was a mass of stings and excruciating language. The sailorman had enraged his particular bee with smoke till it stung him on the nose, and he was away indoors seeking bluebags. The soldierman developed his customary tactless memories of wild Indian bees, and suddenly I bethought me of the bee-master.

Up the same old dusty road I sped, and sought urgent counsel at his hands.

"Botherin' you be they? Put a nombrelly over 'em for shade till evenin', an' I'll come an' hive 'em for you."

I came back with this judicious counsel, and found the American, who despised alcohol, sipping ice-water with a moody and resentful eye on the quince tree. In the evening the bee-master came, removed the umbrella which had shaded the swarm, and hived it with a quiet skill which the American, in his obstinate intelligent way took to heart and has repeated many times since without a sting or swear-word. But he was a bloated poor thing, and secured a lot of cossetting from the females of the house.

Came a day when the meagre war breakfast-table was brilliant with a fragrant comb of our own honey; the expensive glucose, miscalled honey, which the unhappy, unlearned city dweller buys, has no chance with those who keep bees in the garden of experience and know the taste of honey gathered from flowers in the dew of the dawn and the sunshine of noon; nothing less for them than the perfumed sweetness of lime and clover, with the later harvest of deep-coloured heather-honey, rich in its unmistakable aromatic flavour.

In the autumn time of planting garden bloom every bee-lover should manage to have long edgings of sage and hyssop and thyme; they are all lovely bloomers, easy to grow and much beloved by bees. A combination full of nectar is snapdragon and catmint; one cannot have too many snapdragons for bees, nor of the pretty little hardy border annual, "gilia tricolour"; or that other hardy annual, the godetia; *Limnanthes Douglassii* is a nectar-bearer too.

The autumnal Michaelmas daisies should be in the bee garden ; on a sunny day Canterbury Bells always hum with a merry throng of foragers about their clappers ; in spring they seek for crocuses, arabis, wallflowers, tulips, and all the early pollen-bearers. On light soil bee-keepers grow standards and bushes of snowy mespilus, as it is a great nectar-bearer, and the honey from it is of a peculiarly delicate flavour.

The little intimate happenings of the garden sway our household temper in a remarkable degree ; the rhythms of indoor life respond electrically to the pulse of varied life outside ; a good hatch of chicks in the early spring, the birth of a brace of handsome kids ; the first-found thrushes' nest, the new litter of kittens ; the early stir of bee-life at crocus time ; a hundred little glad events accent the march of days and swell the human happiness that attends them.

It is the gardener who is generally the bearer of good tidings ; he comes in with a studied effort at phlegm, watching our faces to see what his news will do to us ; but to be frank he deceives us little, for an irradiance of pleasure always struggles through his naïve affectation of calm. . . . " I've got something to show you," he will say, and we process into the pine and bracken to behold what this new joy may be.

How do people live in towns when there is all this happiness in a garden ?

The next year's swarm provided us with an occurrence of great rarity; one which promised phenomenal luck. One morning as I was catching my train to go to London and do the daily wartime office-penance, I saw a stir of great activity round the bee-village. I was vexed.

"It looks like a swarm," I said, and the gardener agreed. Among his many accomplishments he does not number bee-lore. Like most men of his calling he rather dislikes bees, because they chase him about at his work. The way bees and gardeners antagonise each other used to puzzle me until I learned the very simple explanation. It seemed unnatural that he who serves orchard and flower-bed should upset the little creatures who depend on these things for existence. But I have heard too many gardeners say the same thing to doubt the fact that the antipathy is common. In the course of learning all I could about bees, I found at last that they greatly dislike human perspiration; and one only has to reflect on the arduous work a gardener often does to see the meaning of it all.

"When I'm mowing they won't leave me alone." One often hears the grievance.

I looked, therefore, at the darting, singing throng about the hives that sunny morning with some concern.

"I don't suppose you can do anything," I said, rather ungraciously, and went off to town, wishing the bees had had the tact to wait till the next day, which, being Saturday, would have given me a chance to attend to matters.

The good-hearted man was stung by these words to extreme valour. My astonishment was very great when I found on return at night that three swarms had come out during the day, and that he had taken them all and put them ready for hiving. I reflected on this service with more than ordinary gratitude, and during dinner there was lively controversy as to what should be done with the bees.

They were not true swarms but only "casts," and some were for returning them to the parent hives—which could easily have been done, for the faithful valiant had betrayed great intelligence in his work, labelling each bunch with the number of the hive it had come from. But the majority vote went to combining the three and hiving them on the upper lawn, where stood one of the fine hives our American soldier had built last year; now resplendent in white paint and fully furnished with frames, brood wax, and super of sections, complete.

My mind misgave me as I pictured three rival queens fighting within for supremacy; but I was over-persuaded and shown clearly that the combined hordes would make a very good start for our empty hive, with a fair chance to breed up a colony strong enough to winter successfully; and do fine work next spring. So we set out in the scented dusk, and shook three buzzing masses on to the board leading up to the hive, enjoying to the full that pleasing moment in bee-craft when one sits around to watch the orderly ranks, gorged with honey, go marching up into their new quarters.

But next morning she who was sweeping up fallen rose-petals below the terrace, burst in upon us with the news:

"I think the new hive is coming out!"

I remembered the three queens and went forth with renewed misgiving. The air was thick with flying bees, and there was no manner of doubt as to their intention. They were "coming out" with a vengeance. Three queens were too much of a good thing, and the whole community had struck. They were flying high, too, and meant to get away. Before we had time to fetch the garden syringe and shower them with a fine cooling spray, they had gone off to a neighbouring garden down the hill, and settled in the topmost bough of a high pear tree.

Much concerned, and in a great hurry, the gardener accepted the peasant's advice to "ting 'em"; fetching bits of old brass, frying-pans, fruit cans, even an old copper warming pan, and thrust one into every available hand, for us to beat with stones. The village folk beat their discordant tattoo in perfect faith, but I can never decide if there is anything in it. Does the ecstatic sensitive throng overhead respond to the vibration of the air . . . do they feel the thrill of the disturbance in their ether home? Or is it really only the survival of an old English law of trespass which says you may follow your bees on to anyone's ground and collect them, if you have warned them noisily first that a swarm is abroad, and if you keep it in sight all the time it is flying. You may not lose your swarm, hear neighbourly news of its whereabouts later in the day, and then go and collect it, without permission from the owner of the property.

We ting'd industriously away, to be on the safe side, while the peasant owner of the pear revolved round his tree with sympathetic concern, staring hopelessly aloft. "You must 'ave a bushel o' bees theer," he volunteered, and then, consolingly, "They cooden be in a worser place."

Half-heartedly I collected the smoke-bellows, veil, and swarm-box, and called for a ladder. But the gardener endeared himself to all stout hearts for ever by refusing to allow me up. "It's no place for you. I'll do it," said he, and I thankfully became an onlooker. His wife girded him for battle, and finally we saw an armoured figure disappear into the far high branches. His coat sleeves were tied at the wrists with string and his trousers at the ankle, his hat was veiled in black net, his hands stoutly gloved.

The ladder was lashed, the swarm sheet spread on the ground, and, to cut a long story short, when he got to the top he could not reach the cluster, which hung giddily on a slender bough, and in trying to get at it, shook it abroad instead of into the box. Instantly the air was alive with a whirling throng, and presently, to our complete despair, we saw the whole contingent gather together and disappear down the valley.

We gathered the bee paraphernalia together and stole sorrowfully home. The emptied hive sang loud of our loss in its vacant silence; we had a depleted, aching feeling, and the gardener himself was untiring in self-rage. He had done his best, but he hated to fail, and tramped miles around, asking near and far for news of the lost swarm, without success. Beekeepers are very kind to one another. Everyone was most sympathetic, but none could help; and toward nightfall I saw a bronzed, dejected face set off wearily homeward. I was so sorry for him that I almost forgot to miss the bees; but not quite, for they have a strange way of furnishing one's life. The ardent insect community, with its bitter laws and exquisite rewards, cannot live under human observation without earning a great deal of human love.

As night drew on the "outdoor squad" of my household began to gather its blankets and pillows and settle itself in the hammocks for the ultimate luxury of a garden, sleeping out. The moon rolled higher in high heaven, making her own peculiar glory, and the light breeze swayed us where we hung between the pines. I heard one sleepy voice lament, " I wish we had not lost those bees " ; and drifted into slumber with renewed grieving.

And in the morning that happened which makes the peasants through the valley still smile upon us in congratulation! Being Sunday, no one hurried up ; we talked lazily while we watched the squirrels darting overhead, and the little birds splashing in the bird-bath on the lawn ; presently a tense, high sound made us one and all alert . . . from far off the thrilling sound of bees. . . .

" Another swarm ? " we questioned, wondering, and sat up to peer anxiously down the garden slope.

Below the wood we saw them, streaming back across the valley in a golden hymning flood ; our bees coming back to us !

As they passed over each cottage the village folk came out to cry and marvel. Unbelieving, breathless, astounded, we watched the miracle. Straight, straight back they came to us, and as they reached the hives the stream divided into three, and each swarm returned to its own particular hive.

To lose a swarm and then have it return is reckoned the greatest possible omen of good luck in village lore. We were inclined at the moment to walk a trifle loftily among our fellows, since we

"As they passed over each cottage the village folk came out to cry and marvel." *Chap. VIII.*

had not one, but three swarms return. We felt that luck so unusual must be more than luck ; it must be a fortune, and when it comes we won't be mean, we will be generous to everyone and keep bees all our lives.

The sailorman says it must mean that his valuable services will be so appreciated that a rich merchant will cast an eye on him when the war is over, see his great worth and embosom him as a partner in some lordly shipping offices in the West End of London ; the disabled gunner with curly hair, silk socks, and an overdraft at his bank, thinks his play will be accepted by Mr. Harwood and produced amid thunders of acclaim at the Ambassadors Theatre ; the war-baby yells for Glaxo and gets his luck immediately ; the General looks yearningly after a tall woman whom he has wooed long and vainly, but surely means to win ; the supple girl who does morris dancing for us at time of full moon glances at the sailor, and twingles of fearful apprehensive joy glimmer across his brows in the midst of all his joyous prophetic clamour of the way he thinks good luck will come to him. He falters as though dimly discerning it might even take another form.

The golden-haired Heart o' Joy sits silent on the edge of her hammock, till we ask her what her luck is to be. "I don't know," she confesses ; "but I am going to write to the American right away to tell him of his, which is that he's going back to

California covered with honours and without a wound. He must surely have the best luck of all because he made the hives."

"Perhaps she'll get the best because she can't guess it," murmurs the gunner, watching her wistfully.

"And my luck will be a trip all round the world as soon as war is over. I feel it in my bones," I sing out, gathering pillows and blanket *en route* for house and breakfast.

With the exception of their wayward impulses at swarming time, the bees may be considered "domesticated animals," I think. At any rate, they inhabit the houses built for them, as the chickens and dogs and goats do, and it is only when the sun and summer go to their heads that they try to resume the free manners of a wild state. A wise beekeeper knows how to control that misguided lust and even beginners like ourselves can learn to turn it to advantage.

But no one can call the birds of the garden domestic animals; not even though they use the bird-bath daily and make little nests in the round boxes nailed on to the tree-trunks for them, not even when they sidle up at tea-time and ask for crumbs as our tame robin does. Even so, even with all this acceptance of human attention, the birds remain splendidly wild.

It was eight or nine years ago, in a snowy spell,

that we first conceived the idea of a bird-yard. The little creatures were hard put to it for food. They would cluster about the windows spent and hungry, till we swept a bare patch on the gravel path and sprinkled grain, breadcrumbs, bacon rind, scraps of meat, and hard-boiled egg for them (easy, generous pre-war days). The congregation of pretty creatures pleased us all so much that we decided to teach them to know one special spot as their own dedicated feeding ground.

When the frost broke, we paved a small " yard " in front of the raven's cage, and bought an unpretentious terra-cotta bird-bath from the neighbouring pottery. Upon the bricked place we daily sprinkled offerings to the birds; snails, worms, caterpillars, and house tit-bits with, every morning, a libation of sparkling water, poured out in the shallow bath-bowl.

The bird-yard was well within view of the house windows, and we learned a great deal about our dainty guests; they took all we did for them with the best possible grace, frequenting their corner whenever the coast was clear. I regret to say that the cats very soon learned to ambush near by, and Dandy liked drinking from the sun-warmed bath a great deal better than his own brown glazed bowl with " Drink, puppy, drink " written on it. However, with the exception of these drawbacks the birds found their special pitch highly desirable.

There would congregate, in animated chat and quarrel, pied wagtails, song-thrushes, blackbirds, robins, starlings, sparrows, ringdoves, tits, jays, fieldfares, and mistle-thrushes. The jolliest little fellows I truly think are the chaffinches. Very early in the year they will begin to ripple out their pretty spring song, so fresh and joyous.

About March the breasts of the cock birds are burning bright, an ardent flush glows over their feathers, and their manners correspond to this tell-tale change. They leave their bachelor parties, clubs, diggings chambers, and what-not, where they have roistered and foregathered in masculine exclusiveness all autumn and winter, and turn their attention violently to wooing the fair sex.

During this fevered time they are the most quarrelsome little fellows in the world, scrapping with each other in the intervals of their urgent troubadouring. They sing a very clear song, three calls . . . "Moll-moll-moll," and then a scale run, quick and tripping, which sounds just like "kiss-me-dear." If we listen carefully to the different efforts of each one we can find a distinct individuality in expression. Some are much more tender than others.

There was one brave fellow we got to know quite well, because he had a bent feather in his tail which stood up at a ridiculous angle, and his "kiss-me-dear" would have melted the heart of a stone.

"The long hair interfered with her play." *Chap. VII.*

"Dandy likes drinking from the bird-bath better than from his own bowl."
Chap. VIII.

He won his demure little brown lady, and they made a lovely nest in the old dust-bin full of sticks that had a hole in its side, and I am sorry to say Tatty-Bogle ate one of their children before it could quite fly. Doubtless the two have now separated again after the labours of parenthood, and are trapseing the countryside in care-free communities of nuns and monks.

The chaffinches appear to lead a blissful married life, for though the men-folk are so quarrelsome among their rivals in wooing-time, they share the domestic life which supervenes as if they enjoy it. A complete contrast to some others, ostriches, for instance. I was deeply interested once, to find that Mr. Ostrich was a henpecked husband, when I had wandered very far from my garden to stay with a girl-friend.

I had known her first in a City office. She was then on the editorial staff of a paper, since defunct, which emanated from dingy and ill-ventilated premises. Amid that dust her face bloomed fresh and sweet as a wild rose; I used to look for the smile in her blue eyes as a thirsty traveller looks for a spring of cool water, whenever I would betake myself down her alley-way, coyly attempting to peddle my wares. In those early days of a literary career most editorial offices seemed like armed and frowning fortresses, but to hers I could go without fear of rebuff, sure that however little or much I might sell of poems, articles or what-nots, I would get a friendly welcome.

Many years afterwards I found myself sitting on the wide verandah of her African home. A dashing young South African Lochinvar had seen and wooed her Saxon beauty and transplanted her overseas. Their property stretched far on every hand, set in a fertile valley ringed with blue mountains and rich in the inestimable boon of water. With water one can make anything grow in that wonderful country. We who scratch and scrape in the thin worn-out soil of England have little idea of the overflowing wealth that waits our wooing in the rich silt of some of those African valleys.

From the cool shade of the stoep I sat and watched the sun-stricken landscape in deep content. A warm and heavy perfume puffed from the mimosa thorn in lazy gusts, as though a sleepy priest swung a giant censer. On the table beside me my hostess had piled a great bloomy bowl of nectarines, peaches, and Muscatel grapes, with the latest novels to entertain me, while she went calling across the veldt. In the distance I could see her hooded Cape cart roll steadily along. From the back of the house soft, muffled sounds told me the black servants had finished their siesta. Rich flats of lucerne lay gleaming before me, far and wide, green as May meadows in an English spring.

Some of them had been cut into long pens very

much like suburban gardens at home, an idea assisted by the absurd little lean-to of hurdles erected in each "lot" for the married ostriches.

The birds intrigued me much. I watched them with immense interest during the whole of my visit. Each wedded couple was allowed a house and garden to itself, and very interesting it was to watch the endearments of the newly wedded couples. One surveyed a most Utopian prospect— a series of Edens inhabited by billing and cooing Adams and Eves. Towards laying time, however, a change came o'er the scene, for Mrs. Ostrich would suddenly develop into a screaming, tearing virago. All these sentimental-eyed wives, who had sighed and coquetted, preened and smirked like lovesick misses, turned round on their besotted spouses in the most amazing and revolting way. They gave the poor fellows no peace, chasing them from pillar to post, fighting, nagging, worrying, till the wretched grooms were utterly subdued by want of sleep and food. Having reduced them to the extreme of docility, they then insisted that they should take their place on the nests at night, and for the sake of peace, doubtless, rather than from any keen paternal sense, the male ostriches settled themselves down in their villa residences every night on the stroke of the hour to cuddle the eggs and give their wives a rest. Through the cool nights under the great burning African stars these sensible wives would roam the lucerne, stretch their pink legs, and regard, without emotion, their broken-spirited mates.

There was one exception, however, to this, which excited my wonder not a little. Among the orderly rows of pens I would frequently notice one bride languishing by the wire fence and gazing into the next run, while the ardent wooing of her bridegroom fell on deaf ears. I was so interested in her irregular habits that at last I pointed her out to my pretty hostess, who instantly explained the lady's trouble. Her mate, it seemed, had been plucked before being put into the breeding pen, and, as far as her wayward fancy was concerned, he might as well not have been there at all. The great white plumes which sell so well in the northern markets grow on the wings and tails of ostriches at mating time, and must serve some seductive purpose, as it is an absolute fact that the wretched bird utterly refused to look at her bridegroom, who was deeply in love with her, because he had no great bunches of white feathers to add zest to his wooing. She spent the whole of her time looking over the fence at her neighbour's husband (who pursued his marital career with the usual garnishments) in an agony of thwarted passion.

To return to Surrey.

The gaudy jays are very common here. Their screaming cry is part of the country sound and would leave a blank if it were missing. The thrushes take the snails from the bird-yard and tap them on the nearest sharp-edged stone till the shell is broken, when they eat the spluttering contents: a nasty chilly meal it looks.

The starlings are much admired units in the motley crew at breakfast-time. Their rich bronze-blue plumage, spangled with gold flecks, is very handsome, and their stubby shape without any elegant long tail feathers is very distinctive. We have a family of them every year in the top story of the dove-cote, bare now of the magpie pigeons we used to keep; because corn was too hard to get in war-time. They are very imitative birds, and have already learned to copy the cat-whistle which brings obedient pussies trooping anxiously homeward from every part of the garden.

Although our bird-bath answers all practical purposes, I would not care to advocate it as one of beauty. Indeed, I am always hoping for the day when I can find a nice old one in carved stone to take its place. I found a friend hunting Bond Street for a bird-bath one day and led him firmly away from daylight robbery. I introduced him instead to the sculptor, who made him a very interesting piece of garden work. The boy is in lead and the bath is in stone. The idea is rather a jolly one. It is called "The Divining Rod," and the boy is a fairy boy, who has been playing on a heap of oak leaves and acorns till he has magicked one leaf bigger than himself. He is kneeling on his enchanted oak leaf with a hazel twig in his hand ; he has been " divining " for the water, which rain, dew, or fairy magic has produced for his benefit in the curve of the leaf.

I must confess my little terra-cotta bowl looks a tame effort after that ;—the only thing is, the birds do bathe and drink in mine, but I hear from my friends that their birds seem to mistake the use of the sumptuous convenience splendidly erected for them, and will insist on perching on the boy's head, despitefully using it, instead of bathing in the leaf as they were intended to do.

CHAPTER VIII

THE KINGDOM OF PAN

There is no house possessing a goat but a blessing abides therein.
MAHOMET.

AS the great European war pressed more and more heavily upon the belligerent countries, we in our quiet corner of a guarded Isle with the rest of our fellow Britons saw the bogey of starvation gibbering at us. I had to preside over a jamless, butterless, meatless breakfast table where the porridge was served dry and the coffee black. The only things that seemed to retain their ancient quality were the sun and the silver, which shone as merrily as ever they did; but the provisions vanished one by one and at last even the china began to take on a hybrid appearance as we had to replace it with other patterns, for the Germans had overrun the Luneville potteries in France and we were no longer able to obtain the pretty ware which had pleased our eyes for years.

In the long, long ago I was trained at the greatest Maternity Hospital in the world, the Rotunda, Dublin, where I acquired a respect that borders on veneration for milk as a food factor. The virtues of good clean wholesome milk were so ingrained into my conscience by the time I acquired a diploma that I never failed to see to it thereafter that anybody who came under my care either as patient, dependent or guest was daily supplied with the best milk and butter obtainable. Fresh and creamy it appeared o' mornings with the coffee and porridge and at later meals in puddings, junkets, cakes and creams; in one form or another milk was always to the fore.

It was during the Great War that I suspect many women became aware of a possession in themselves which for lack of a better word I must call a housewives' conscience; that protection which wells up and flows from her; the mother-instinct safeguarding her household, her trust. It is the same care which spreads in ever-widening ripples through the whole community, from the housewife in her home, from the mayor in his township, and from the king in his kingdom. When I found that the shortage of milk had become so acute that we could not even get it tinned, my housewife's conscience was mightily distraught; this little fortress I guarded must surely be supplied with something in the nature of milk or I was failing in my trust; meat we obtained in tiny rationed quantities, and supplemented with what eggs we could gather from our starveling fowls; for sugar we substituted honey from our hives. But the loss of milk was a desperate affair.

It was at this juncture that Master Holmes Pegler burst forth in the columns of the Daily Press as the gospeller of the goat. It was the " poor man's cow " he said, and I recalled the scrubby creatures whose silly faces I had seen biting gorse on the village commons from time to time ; melancholy, shaggy little things they seemed, whose milk I had always believed was smelly, and tasted nasty, and gave Malta fever to those who drank it.

I had heard, somewhere, that asses' milk was in vogue among invalids and infants, and pondered gloomily on the possibility of acquiring somewhere a milky she-ass. Relief came from the remote trenches of France. The lassie, faithfully fulfilling her national duty of cheering a lonely soldier, mentioned in her weekly letter to our American warrior the council of despair reached by the despised Pegler. That all-wise youth replied that in the West where he came from goats were infinitely more venerated than cows, and in course of some weeks sent, to illumine our ignorance, a copy of a Californian monthly magazine called *The Goat World* in which we learnt to our exceeding astonishment that goats' milk was sweeter and richer than any other, and that Malta fever was unheard of outside Malta, where the natives do not apparently understand the first principles of cleanliness.

Thus encouraged we cast about to obtain a nanny; the lass roamed the countryside enquiring through wood and wold, to find that other people appreciated the blessings of the creatures and were loath to part with them; but ultimately for four pounds she acquired a tall virago with long horns, and a revolting habit of butting everyone who approached her, preferably when their backs were turned, and her advent caused a considerable flutter in the domestic circle.

Returning from London Town that evening I found an interested party sitting round watching the habits of this new acquisition; she was tethered on the croquet lawn, not yet dug up for potato growing, where she had baaed forlornly and gnawed grass as if it would break her heart to leave a blade.

A neighbouring peasant taught us how to milk, and thereafter my household had its five pints of fine new milk daily and my housewife conscience was at peace; her offering made so great a difference to the short war-rations that we grew to value our nanny-goat; and, avoiding her horns, would find much to admire in her calm ruminant eye, her ever-wagging beard and the rich bag full of blessing with its two long teats.

She took on the lustre of a benefactor and made but the most reasonable demands upon domestic economy; she eat grass, leaves, gorse, broom, boughs of trees, flowers, vegetables, roots, ivy, anything she could find on the steep valley pasture, asking us only for water, rock-salt, some oats, and a shelter to run to when it rained. She fed fastidiously on only the cleanest of these meats, utterly refusing to touch and scarcely smelling at anything that had been trampled or mired; we learned that, compared to a goat, the cow is a very unclean feeder.

Our friends refreshed with creamier junkets than ever before chorussed great praise of "the poor man's cow"; we named our nanny "St. Holmes," and the morris dancer spent a gorged and joyous afternoon drawing a picture of a stained-glass window containing the haloed portrait of the now much-admired Holmes Pegler, who first turned our thoughts in the right direction.

But one day an officer's wife called, saying she was quartered near by and heard we kept goats; might she buy some milk for her baby who was delicate? We could not well refuse to let a baby share our milk, so we halved the frothing bowl night and morning with great goodwill, learning in due course that the baby had picked up and was thriving apace.

A few weeks later an urgent call came from over the hill from another mother—her baby was dying; she heard we kept goats; might she have some milk to save her baby's life? That was a call no one might refuse, so we gave all we had and I cast about to find more goats.

By this time they were in great demand all over England and difficult to obtain, but after long travail I obtained two—one from a rich Society woman who charged me twelve pounds for a non-pedigree nanny with such a congested udder that one side of it was useless, the other from a well-meaning friend for eight pounds, and it proved to be a non-breeder. So the household supplies became short once more.

At this moment the sanctified Pegler once more hurled himself into the breech—revealing to a purblind public the fact that there was in existence a body called the British Goat Society, which keeps a Herd Book and register of pedigree stock, holds yearly shows to encourage goat-breeding on the lines of deep-milking records, and advertises animals for sale among its members. I joined the Society and discovered an astonishing number of facts about the formerly despised beast. That goats' milk is much more digestible than cows', for instance, containing 5·14 per cent of butter-fat as against 3·13 per cent in cows, and that tuberculosis, from which about a third of milch cows suffer, is absolutely unknown to the goat.

One Mr. Powell Owen has a remarkable table based on extensive investigations conducted all over the Continent into the causes of mortality among infants during their first year of life, the figures of which bring out the astonishing fact that

THE KINGDOM OF PAN

the death-rate is smaller in every district where a greater number of goats is kept.

For instance, the total number of goats kept in Suabia is 7,325, and the death-rate 35·4 per cent. In Palatine where 52,500 goats are kept the death-rate is 17·6 per cent. Again, consider the following: In Hesse, where 10·6 goats are kept per 100 inhabitants, the death-rate is down to 15·3 per cent, and in Wurtemberg, where only 3·8 goats are kept per 100 inhabitants, the death-rate leaps to 21·7 per cent.

Armoured in this interesting knowledge I diligently betook myself to my first B.G.S. show and learned there what a magnificent animal a well-bred, well-groomed, deep-milking goat can be—with her great well-spring ribs, coat of satin, slender legs, small hornless head, and silken bag yielding a gallon of milk and more a day. I learned there that the goat is by no means the humble, indeed, almost absurd beast of the village common I had supposed it, but is highly valued, highly priced, and highly bred by a large number of people in these animal-loving islands.

The rich, creamy milk is growing yearly more appreciated, and the ideal of every intelligent breeder is to breed for quantity and quality of milk. More than one enthusiast says the day will come when we breed and show twelve-quart milkers! In California the two-gallon goat, it seems, is no unusual figure in well-kept herds. The feed of a goat is so much cheaper than that of a cow that it seems a pity everyone does not have one, and solve the ever-recurring question of the home milk supply.

I noticed at this show, where I was being intensively educated, many faces well-known to me of old in the dog-breeding world; and commenting on this to one well-known owner of world-famous kennels I found that puppies reared on goats' milk suffer hardly at all from worms, and develop fine bone. A breeder of any good stock is almost invariably impatient of owning anything scrub, so it followed that doggy people, to whom this tip was well known, bred good goats as well as good dogs.

Much excited by this adventure into new worlds of knowledge, I roamed round and round the show ring, watching the beautiful creatures being led in and judged, and growing hourly more and more dissatisfied with my scrub stock at home;—obviously it were better to have one heavy milker than three indifferent ones. Presently a short woman stopped near me to speak to a judge, she was smoking a cigarette and both her smoke and loud voice drifted across my senses—" Oh! I've been getting rid of my rubbish," she said; and a cold sensation almost like suspicion trickled down my back. I asked someone near by who she was, " That? Oh! that's Lady —— "

So I saw in the flesh the wealthy woman who had sold me her " rubbish " for twelve pounds.

THE KINGDOM OF PAN

Later I met a goat-breeder who was a human being before a trader, and from her I bought, for fifteen pounds, a full herd-book nanny-goat mated to a herd-book aristocrat, and shortly due to kid. Seldom has a little house received a new friend with more pomp and circumstance.

Tossing her dainty head she minced down the garden way like a queen in Grand Opera; proudly led by the gardener who strove vainly to subdue the glitter in his eye, and followed in admiring array by the whole household, war-baby and all. When pastured out in the field she struck admiration from every passing bosom, for no one could fail to see the challenging tale of breed in every line of her.

To my profound pleasure she was what is known as an Anglo-Nubian-Toggenburg, my choice had been necessarily limited by my purse, and dearly had I hoped to find a pedigree goat to start me with a herd whose strain might combine just that strong threefold strand. The heavy Swiss Toggenburgs are noted for their great quantity of milk, the slender racy Nubians for the richness of quality in theirs, and the English strain stands for acclimatisation and constitution. So that in an A.N.T. one gets, or should get, the ideal goat.

Shortly after her arrival our treasure bestowed two handsome kids upon us, with dainty little hornless heads and beautiful Nubian flop-ears like orchidpetals, who gambolled their way to every heart among the golden gorse and sweet field-clover. And we learned, once and for all, the wisdom of keeping a well-bred goat, for our new nanny gave us more milk than all the other three had done together.

A blue-eyed gardener sat herself down to transscribe these happenings overseas, and at his first leave the American soldier came hurtling back to "make goat-stalls." He found us in pleased possession of *The Book of the Goat*, by that same Holmes Pegler, whom having not seen we yet greatly loved, and in its pages he discovered a full prescription for magnificent housing accommodation.

Thereupon ascended once more from this peaceful spot the hymn of his saw and plane. Day and night, working with hideous ardour, he wrought against time, till I fled the garden which sounded like a place of wrath; and even the war-baby, who toddled after him in fatuous admiration, was buried and lost in shavings.

After he had gone back to France, and the incredible blessings of silence flowed once more over the home, I emerged to see what he had done, and found my beautiful goats stalled like princes. A most astonishing fellow. I wonder if all young Americans are as swift, as noisy, as compelling, and as clever.

Not long afterwards the gardener was to be seen at an unseemly hour in a stiff and spotless linen

THE KINGDOM OF PAN

coat leading the two kids groomed and elegant, with their tiny polished hoofs clattering merrily over the tiled garden path, to catch a train for Guildford Show. And then the family party set off on the long spin through Moor Park, where Swift met Stella and loved her long ago; past Waverley Abbey, where Scott never wrote a line; over the long Hog's Back with the "coloured counties" stretched far on either hand to Guildford town and Stoke Park. The carefully bred horses, cattle, sheep and goats of the countryside were out in spruce array to compete for challenge cups, prizes of money, honour and glory; and their owners were out for the fun of a sporting day.

The-Only-Woman-in-the-World carried a homely basket of sandwiches and fruit; the Only-Mother-she-has carried a camera and notebook. The rest of the party, being guests and care-free, carried light hearts and a certain lay-out of bets between them as to the winnings of the home brace.

We made straight for the goat end of the Park, where sundry large tents, bespangled with hurdles, class numbers, chains and feed, held the bleating exhibits.

Once again we said to ourselves, "What nice things goats are!" And how can they be bred up from the horrible hairy things one sees chewing grass, gorse and string on the commons to the slim-legged satin-coated, fine-lined beauties of a first-class herd ? There is all the difference between the two that you can find between a peach and a potato.

As the cold wind died away, I began to roam from tent to tent in happy dreaming mood. Here was a ring full of heavy-boned Swiss nannies, mouse-coloured, or black-and-white ; or pure white Saanen goats, with great milk-bags of silken texture and calm ruminant faces. There never seems anything challenging or racy about Toggenburg or Saanen goats. They are broad-headed handsome mother-things ; gentle and unexciting ; the people who love them seem to be kind and calm too. I watched Mr. Bryan Hook judging them. He works with fatalistic unhurried calm ; he knows what he admires, and to that he awards the prize. He does not dip and hover and flutter over the fraction of an inch difference in the length of an ear or the profile of a nose like the Nubian judges sometimes do ; he wants big well-made goats, who give large quantities of milk, and to that end he observes the animals. Watching him judge is like eating when hungry, or sleeping when tired. One does not question, one accepts his judgment and reposes within it.

The new exhibitors, rank novices, scurried about like water-spiders, tentative and timorous ; eyeing the fortunate with unconscious pathos ; petting their disgraced fondlings at surreptitious moments in furtive desperate loyalty and waking in me for one a passionate sympathy. I know so very well how they felt. They with their mistakes, their hopes, their enthusiasm, their good-hearted desire to win, and the humble way they submit to being pushed aside and disregarded by the old-time hardened winners, are food for endless thought, observation and entertainment. I am an old-time exhibitor in other fancies and had long passed the horrors of first showing; but found here in the goat-world, the same as in every other, the infinite entertainment of fellow-humans.

A solemn moment transpired after lunch when a tall interesting-looking man lingered by our kids to comment and admire; he spoke with such authority that I asked his name; the lass-I-love with a cauliflower in either hand at which two velvet muzzles were ardently chewing nearly fell on her knees to learn that this was Holmes Pegler, the family Saint, before her eyes in flesh and blood. Not all the prizes of America and Europe combined could have wrought a sterner pride within her than his generous word of praise.

As his thoughtful melancholy visage melted away into the busy crowds, it seemed to me as if the speechless adoration of the group he left behind must surely beat like a burning ray into his back.

One of our kids was called Domino for she was a sleek black thing spotted with white; a most arresting animal when seen grazing on a cloth-of-emerald pasture; either side of her shapely hornless head hung long white ears streaked with black, and she had a way of standing with her legs wide spread like horses do at shows, which gave her a very well-bred and racy appearance. When she was born the gardener was so depressed at her unusual colouring that he hung his head and almost whispered the news, as if he were admitting a family scandal; I hurried off to welcome the new arrivals and see what this strange thing might be. The beautiful mother baaed exultantly in welcome and strutted round her run, nuzzling and kissing her babies with the utmost pride and joy.

The little billy was a handsome and exact replica of herself, a neat strawberry roan with long white flop ears like orchid petals, but the nanny-kid was a showy damsel, dressed in stylish black with big spots and splotches of white all over the place; under both their chins hung little white tassels, tribute to the cross of Swiss in their blood, pretty little useless furry tassels that bobbed with every movement like the bells their Alpine forebears wore round their necks as they roamed the mountain pastures. The little miss eyed me timidly, begging for approval, and utterly won my heart away.

"Isn't she lovely?" I breathed, and the gardener mopped his brow in amazed relief. He was a bit shocked, I could see, at my admiring such loud apparel, but thankful as well.

"Wait a bit," I said, "I will see what the book

"Domino, the spotted kid." *Chap. IX*

"The war baby . . . Over our tender task we re-modelled the world. . . ." *Chap. III*

says." And ran indoors to consult the faithful Pegler, where I discovered a picture of " Bricket Cup," a great Anglo-Nubian winner who was so exactly like my new kid that I made hurried search along her pedigree and found what I suspected.

"She has thrown back to her Eastern blood," I ran back to say to the much-interested man, and together, deeply pleased and proud, we studied the picture of her magnificent ancestor.

"She's the very spit of him," he declared, and from that hour Domino took pride of place in the valley, for her marking was too remarkable to pass unnoticed and every comment brought forth the story from the gardener, who was her champion ; confronting unbelievers with both the book and her pedigree.

"Reminds me of the story of Jacob in the Old Testy-man, she do ; I always doubted the spots and stripes in his flocks and herds but now I can believe anything of they Eastern goats."

Being an energetic and gamesome lad we called the billy kid Dynamo ; he was his mother's favourite, for while Domino would walk straight to the fount of refreshment and help herself, Dynamo would always go to her first and kiss her soft kind muzzle with his little eager tongue, and after this graceful act go and drink lustily, his tail racing like anything.

She looked for his kisses, and let him suckle long after she had weaned Domino with buttings and baa-ings. As he grew up she let him steal her corn now and again, a tremendous favour, for healthy goats love their stomachs ;—someone once told me they have seven of them, which might account for the hobby.

Towards Awe-time our Dynamo began to announce his progress to manhood by a musky smell, which reminded me of the smell of the roots of Crown Imperial lilies with a sub-smell of tansy. We gave him bachelor quarters, and as the breeding season had now arrived I went far afield one day to see a famous dagger billy-goat to whom I wished to wed my nannies. A "dagger" is a he-goat owning a dam who was a star-milker, and a sire whose dam was also the produce of a milking-prize winner. As the milking qualities so greatly desired by every earnest goat-breeder are handed down through the male line, every stud goat who has a dagger (†) before his name is exceedingly popular, and his kids command a good price.

The visit of inspection was a delightful adventure. I seemed to have strayed into the very kingdom of Pan, where handsome girls and stalwart boys shared the cliffs and sun and sea with highly-bred herds of goats. There was something so clean about the whole thing that it left an indelible impression on my mind. Sweet-breathed generous nannies climbed freely from crag and hollow, cropping the harsh, woody, bitter-sweet herbage they so dearly loved;

THE KINGDOM OF PAN

goats sicken on soft lush grass such as cows like best. An atmosphere of merry industry prevailed among the children, whose fine clear skins, elastic muscles, and brilliant eyes bespoke the wholesome purity of the rich milk on which they had been raised.

The lord of the herd was a very splendid fellow, very big and powerfully smelly ; he was all over like a patchwork quilt in brave array of black and white and tan, he had a very haughty Jewish nose, a profile that went in festoons of rich curves, and his ears hung down like silken curtains beside the beautiful head. I much admired him, and arranged a match for my nannies without delay ; while he wandered round us in kindly curiosity filling the breeze with extravagant odours, being shooed away with such vigour by everybody that I became foolish enough to pity his thwarted overtures and I patted him kindly as he passed my way, a most unfortunate act of friendship, for he responded with intense gratitude, rubbing his head joyously against my arm ; so that I was pursued with a strong goat smell for the rest of the day ; and became exceedingly unpopular whenever I went near the house or among my fellows.

The loneliness of this pariah estate wrought upon my nerves after I had been given tea alone in the summerhouse and I went for a long walk over the cliffs to see what the sea-breeze might do to brisk my smell away. It was a glorious evening—the glowing sea and sky made such music in the heart that I forgot time and distance, walking on and on into the west, lost in the delicious wonder of colour.

Presently I found myself in a park where broad tree-set pastures stretched either side and cattle browsed contentedly. Tired and happy I leaned on the iron fencing to dream awhile longer before I must turn back to face the moonrise in the hollow east. And a queer thing happened then, one I shall never quite forget; the sleek bullocks, grazing far and near winded me and came ambling up to inspect; they crowded round curious and approving, wet muzzles passed up and down my arm, sniffing and licking till I was surrounded by large benignant eyes and a forest of curving horns.

It was the goat odour overpowering the human smell of me which made them my friends, which made them love me unafraid of my form; I was one of them; Pan's own creature; one with the fields and the wild life of the woods. Their smooth flanks heaved gently, as they pressed brotherwise around, sweet-breathed and contemplative.

As I trudged the long way back I sniffed myself contentedly. If patting the billy had made my fellows flee from me it had made the animals kin— so that was all right.

As soon as our little boy Dynamo grew up to full billy-hood he was besought to espouse the lady goats of the valley; I heard him sing his love song one day when I saw the gardener coming down the garden with a love-lorn maiden shamelessly baa-ing on a lead, and I knew that nuptials must be in the offing, for Dynamo spied his visitor and serenaded her at once in the beseeching tones of an emotional canary ; a high soprano chant that accorded most incongruously with his virile beard.

With Domino, she of the spots, proudly betrothed to a spotty " dagger " and Dynamo populating the countryside with handsome little Dynamites we began to feel truly patriarchal.

CHAPTER IX

RAIN ON THE HERBS

> Make me over, Mother April,
> When the sap begins to stir !
> Make me man or make me woman,
> Make me oaf or ape or human,
> Cup of flower or cone of fir ;
> Make me anything but neuter
> When the sap begins to stir !
>
> BLISS CARMEN.

STRAIGHT lines of silver stream down upon the green—every yielding blade and leaf receives its cuff from the skies, bends under it and springs up laughing again ; the garden is full of business, taking in stores of precious wet, roots agrab and ·leaf-lungs breathing deep. Across the lawn I see a shiny Sou'wester bending low over some garden work ; now and again the profile of a young rose-face gleams out of the sheltering hat as it twists this way or that about its job. Beautiful hands, firm and slender, full of character move around tiny rootlets. I watch them enthralled and unobserved. I cannot get used to the thing I made ; so comely, so clever, so self-absorbed, a complete and perfect human being, which my own body was privileged to convey to the world.

Sometimes, in the hurly-burly of this busy hospitable echoing house a mother-woman will sort herself out from among my friends and we will commune together in the deep delicious understanding known only to us, who have created. The dew of wonder never quite dries off a mother-heart, her ecstasy lies silent, richly patient, its power and sweetness known secretly, as the locked flowering of her fallow is known to the heart of the field. I pressed my nose against the window looking at the girl, and yielding to a sweet moment.

A man passed between us and the American soldier comes into the room, his great shoulders wet, his hair curled riotously by the rain. He has a tin bowl and a sponge in his hands.

"I've been unlicing the goats," he laughs. "The little wee goats were lousy, ma'am, and I've unliced them."

He looks like a radiant, mischievous boy, repeating the unusual word; watching to see if he can shock me. Soldiers use queer words. He goes back to his pleasing pastime with a fresh supply of quassia chips, and presently the sun struggles out; a glowing rain-washed girl discovers me idling by the window; I am exhorted to come out and smell the sweet herbs. Arm in arm we proceed upon this amiable pilgrimage.

As we linger by one sweet bush and then another we remember "Mr. Zwanny." Some years ago, at the Royal Horticultural Show I had seen a new rhizomatous iris which shot me with mortal envy, a dusky fellow of dingy soft browns and greys, indescribably restful, which I knew on the instant would complete as nothing else a border of cream and bronze and yellow irises where Thunderbolt and Squalens in varieties were grouped for colour. With pangs I then and there disgorged a half-guinea for a slip of the new plant, whose full grand title is "Souvenir de Zwanenburg," and waited for time and tilth to establish him among us.

Since early March this year we have paid "Mr. Zwanny"—for short—ceremonial visits to see what he will do for us; the tiny slip of tuber with a few lank locks of rootlets dangling by either cheek holding up a forlorn spire of green leaf like a toy sword which we committed to earth long ago is now spread into a lusty patch of pale green rush-like leaves, where long stems rich with bud have been luring us Zwannywards for weeks. He was a bit obstinate in unfolding; but the lass reminds me this gentle day of sun and shower must surely have melted his stern heart, so we go to pay our call, gaily gossiping, and are struck suddenly dumb to find him waiting for us, full open in tremulous splendour; our

RAIN ON THE HERBS

very own Mr. Zwanenburg come to our garden to stay, incorporate, tangible, smiling all over his face, the creature of dreams, who lived in the dusk of our hopes and had been seen so variously in so many minds for two whole years through the only mirror he had possessed, the dim blurred picture of my description.

The lass draws her breath, and we stand side by side before our new friend, tingling with welcome and pride in him.

The April sunshine makes the rich tissue of his green-gold falls glimmer fitfully as though powdered with gold dust; splashes of dull purple lie sullenly under the greeny gold, and he wears blonde whiskers on his cheeks, almost carroty they are. Like the echo of a repented sin shadowy blots of paler purple repeat themselves again in the tender grey standards; our "Mr. Zwanny" is a delicate poet, who has met the world and been stained by it, but turned his stains to beauty in the alchemy of his sweet soul.

In the joy of meeting him at last in the flesh, both of us refrain from commenting on the fact that makes him an anachronism in the border he was purposed to adorn, namely, that neither Squalens (called diversely "squallings" and "skwaylens" by the ancient and modern hymnals regarding them) nor Thunderbolt, nor even the cream and yellow flags have yet made a move toward blooming!

He is up and awake long before the rest of the company and will probably have a place all to himself some day, when we feel brave enough to move and divide him.

There is a certain cream-coloured broom which blooms at Mr. Zwanny's hour; tucked away in my heart is a purpose which will materialise about three years hence, a large display of *Cytisus Præcox*, which is the broom's name, and masses of Souvenir de Zwanenburg bowing and scraping in front of her. It will be a wonderful harmony, and in the fullness of garden-time I'll have it. Meanwhile the fellow is making eyes at the simple little blossoms of the rosemary hedge across the bricked path.

We leave him, at length, to look at other flower friends, but we both feel much enriched in our heart's gladness by this new and intriguing companion. As we move under the speckled sunspots of the wood I confide to the expert my scheme for Mr. Zwanny's ultimate establishment in life and learn with gratitude that she approves. Our eyes being somewhat filled with irises for the moment we neglect the hyssop and tarragon we set out primarily to inspect, in order to see how the other irises are getting along.

Florentina is fat with pale buds, and very soon her white banners will flutter forth, the thick border of King of the Blues is marshalled brave with his buds held up like spear-heads. Victor and Beatrice of the

Pallida family are housed honourably alone in the "blue bed"; their rather shoddy pink silk dressing-gowns concealing from untimely frosts the exquisite creatures themselves, give not the slightest hint of the silvery blue raiment in which Victor and Beatrice will come out to look at us in the magical month of May.

Rollicking among the light sand in a perfect ecstasy of rude health the yellow flags laugh at us under the sun. At least their greenery does, for never a yellow has yawned in his sleep. The Queen of May is sleeping too, though the pink thrift edging to her court of purple lupins is well alight. Love o' Jove will be there when her majesty shows herself—and well he may lose his heart at sight of her, for that rosy pink iris is beautifully throned where we have her there, in a kitchen garden border, with pinks and purples at her feet. It took some years to find her right harmony, but now I am well content and look forward to her blooming every year.

Among the Neglecta irises are many striped and veined in violet or blue which makes them quite distinct from the more usual colourings; they are the folk I find most visitors pass by, for their quaint net-like beauty is a thing to learn in an intimate hour, and love for its modesty.

About certain bulbous irises which set forth two or three years ago, in great style, to make a show of blue and mauve in the blue bed after the rhizomes of Victor and Beatrice had become busied with matters of growth and winter storage, and had passed the youthful hour of their bloom, about these said bulbs I regret to say there hovers some scandal. Goodness knows what the poor fools have been up to, but they grow whiter every year, and are not to be called blue any longer by any stretch of imagination, though they called for tremendous admiration when first they bloomed in purple and blue and grey.

The Only-Woman shakes her wise head and says they want iron in the soil. I ponder on the virtues of iron consumed in vast quantities in my youth to make me pink and wonder why it should nowadays be used to make irises blue. There was one Mr. Blaud, I remember, whose large pills I so utterly despised that I used to bury them whenever possible, perhaps to better purpose than I knew especially if there were irises about. We discuss the dissipated appearance of these bulbous irises and conjecture rather hopelessly on their probable appearance this year; we will try them with medicaments and see what happens.

Among the flat stones that surround the lead boy, on his rose-wreathed ball in the flagged garden, a lot of campions have crowded; and we stand admiring the way the rain slips over their soft plush leaves of palest grey; some must come up,

"The flagged garden in summer-time, where a tall tree accents the scene." *Chap. XV.*

declares the lass, to give the "Pax" rose room, but I am deep in memories and pay little attention. I do not like dogma and precept around my lead boy, he is very precious to me, because most people are shocked at him; and so I err on the side of partiality.

If his little impudent fairy heart has called campions to grow round his feet he shall have them, and I can stuff the hungry rose with extra meals of mulch and manure water at odd times.

The disrespectful grimace of my lead boy has straightened many a conventional lip to prim silence as we walk the garden; and I have consoled shocked hearts by assuring them at once that he is the only one of his kind in the world. But people who have read his story in the latest edition of the *Garden of Ignorance* mostly love him, as I do, in spite of his aggravating gesture.

A great waft of sweetness gushes up as we pass the lavender, even the brown old wood of it seems to brim with scent this warm morning; show me the gardener who has borders and beds of flowers only, with never a corner for demure and fragrant still-room herbs, and I know her for a bird of paradise. Like that lovely bird, she is only a gleaming colour scheme, with never a note of song; a glittering dame of fashion with no heart of homely sweetness below.

Every subtle spirit with the temper and twist of a personality will have her herb garden, whatever else she lacks. There is more humour, tradition, use and pleasure in those quiet leaves of very unobtrusive plants than in almost any other branch of garden work.

Our little cottage set deep in pine and bracken, has always its service of aromatic herbs, both fresh and dry. Blankets and furs are stored away in dried herbs, the earthern jars in parlour and study are sweet year after year with potpourri, the salads and cups are cheered with borage, chervil, tarragon, chives; and never a guest but must have found sweet scents upon her pillow or sheets, for we fill the linen cupboard with bunches of lavender every time it comes in bloom.

It may not be amiss to repeat again the recipe for herb mixture, which keeps moth away from clothes and furs. It is so much more pleasant than the usual smelly naphthaline balls that I feel a pleasure in making it better known, especially as it is quite as effective. Take half a pound each of dried rosemary and mint, four ounces each of tansy and thyme, and two tablespoonfuls of fresh ground cloves. Mix these all well together, store in a well-closed box, and scatter the powder lavishly among the things to be stored, in the proper season. No moth will go near them.

Pot herbs are seldom ornamental; they are mostly country folk, sober and suitably clad in homespun greens and browns, brimful of useful powers, generous in giving, but unobtrusive. A lot of sentimental inaccuracies have crept into the modern journalistic attitude toward herbs; old authorities have been quoted and misquoted. What the writers did not know they have generally made up, and discouragement has dogged the efforts of beginners who have blundered in the dusk of their advice. It is a pity, because herbs are easy to grow, have, many of them, a most sincere and appealing beauty, and play a really large part in the pleasant direction of a country home. They have distinct properties, and the old physicians who used them in their possets and draughts were more benefactors than quacks.

Tansy is a very acrid herb, which flies abhor with violent distaste, so that a bunch of it hung in the larder or kitchen is of great use in keeping them away in the hot summer days; balm, camomile, and yarrow make excellent drinks when infused like tea and allowed to cool. They are all good blood tonics and very refreshing. Bay, of course, is invaluable for flavouring jellies, blanc-manges, stews, and all pickles. Sorrel makes a most excellent soup, with a tart clean taste which is indescribably refreshing; the persistent astonishment of Continental cooks at its absence from the English kitchen garden should be a sure indication of its value to the cook-pot.

We grow more than twenty homely herbs—

thyme, parsley, mint, and sage of course, go without saying, in almost every kitchen garden; but it is easy to grow also tansy, balm, bay, borage, bergamot, lavender, rosemary, catmint, chives, tarragon, chervil, camomile, summer-savory, dandelion, fennel, hyssop, sorrel, yarrow and rue. I have them all, and others too, lad's love and wormwood and honesty and feverfew and angelica, and many more, pleasant, quiet, generous friends to house in a garden.

One of our very special friends has an understanding of herb-tea; so various offerings transpire as bed-time approaches; generally about the time that I am to be found seated before a vast blue flame in which I patiently revolve a brass globe full of pale green coffee beans roasting for the morrow's breakfast; such offerings as a silver tankard of yarrow-tea for a maiden who cherishes her complexion; a tall Venetian goblet dusted with gold wherein sparkles lime-tea to soothe the Art Critic to sleep. (Gathering the lime-buds is an anxious affair, for the lime flowers are beset by bees in myriads every fleeting sunny hour.) And a brilliant Bavarian glass of orange-flower tea, with a few fragrant petals sprinkled on the top to woo a smile from his wife's dear face, where are set a pair of the bluest eyes, purple blue like periwinkle flowers.

If a pale gunner is among us, off his feed and slipping a wee in his hard climb back to health

"The lead boy, and the flagged garden in early spring." *Chap.* X.

a brew of dandelion is persuasively passed his way, called Teraxicum Broth, by way of enticement to sharpen his tooth for meal-times. When hair-washing is engaging our attention the big bushes of rosemary are much besieged; first a grand supply of pure rain-water is drawn from the well—the hard tap water blue with alum and lime, for which we pay vast sums to the local water-rate company, is not permitted to embroil and embitter anyone's hair. The soft water is heated and a strong infusion of rosemary tips made like tea with boiling (soft) water, and this is poured over the well-rinsed heads the very last thing before drying. We choose sunny days for shampoo-parties, as the final virtue is to dry the rosemary-scented tresses in the sun and wind, where they acquire under this treatment a wonderful silken gloss and gleam.

April is the month to sow most herbs. April with her suns and showers, her smiling and her grieving, her temperamental skies, and the great uplift to growth of all the myriad young lives trembling at her knee; young April, the lovely month! The month for the happy toil of garden planting, the greatest sowing and planting month of all; April, the wild, inquisitive, rain-washed maiden of the year; the month which jewels its working hours with love-songs of the birds, and crumbles the kindly soil into the tenderest mood for garden work by the beating fairy fingers of the rain. A month of budding lilac and springing green, when the walks and walls hang white and purple with arabis and aubretia, and the gilly flowers toss their ardent perfumes to the shrill spring air of heaven.

It was in an April time of the year that I received my first never-to-be-forgotten lesson in making a seed-bed. When the trained gardener-girl arrived home at last, in the full regalia of the Royal Horticultural Society's Diploma, I became a frequent and most importunate petitioner at the feet of her wisdom; a perfect pestilence I must have been, asking ceaseless questions like an inquisitive child, babbling in season and out of season about gardens and plants. Frankly I looked upon her not so much as my baby grown up, as a gifted stranger replete with knowledge denied to me; one, too, who if persistently tapped might at times gush out little freshets of learning, to be garnered and assimilated with greedy joy.

Very early I piped my wish to learn how to make a seed-bed, and was convoyed down to the kitchen garden one rain-and-sunny April morn, garrulously happy, to learn the trick. I surveyed the figure bearing rake and fork and spade ahead of me with intense pride; a crowned and anointed gardener, no less, about to instruct me in the ritual of a sacrament.

Two packets of seeds were bestowed which I

RAIN ON THE HERBS

bore reverently after her—seeds which we were about to lay upon the wide breast of Earth where presently they would suffer the pang and splendour of a close embrace, be fused and changed in her mysterious fires and come up again as sparkling seedlings to the light of the sun and the sight of our eyes, come up to the rainfall and the starshine, to frost and wind and dew, to revolve in their little bodies the everlasting miracle of life.

I tramped in the rear of the High Priestess, who was busied with more lowly imaginings than these, for presently I was set upon my knees to weed; there were several chubby baby bracken fronds among the weeds which had crept into the good soil of the frame with great cunning; I basely tried to leave them where they were, the curly-headed youngsters looked so playful and innocent it felt like infanticide to pull them out with my trowel. But the stern eye of my child met mine and I hurried up and slew the lot. There were no such sentiments over the couch grass roots, grasping useless fellows, it was a positive pleasure to chase them out of their hidey-holes, and carry each tiniest perfidious atom to the burning heap away in the wood reserved for noxious weeds.

I grew vastly enamoured of the job, reflecting on the beautiful nursery we were preparing for the seeds so lovingly cuddled in our overall pockets. The clean and fresh turned earth looked very enticing and comfortable; I picked out tiny stones, dead leaves, stray rootlets, and every foreign body I could set eyes on with fatuous industry, till a voice rose in admonition.

"Little fibrous roots are good for manure, you know."

I started, guiltily dropping a gleaning, and abated my energies to watch the next ritual which was truly ecclesiastical in its form. The High Priestess herself mounted into the frame and solemnly marched round and round the small space, conscientiously placing each small sturdy footmark close to the last so that presently I saw the loose crumbly soil tramped into a firm flat surface, which we then raked over lightly.

The next request was for a straight bamboo cane, and as I made for the tool shed to espy if such might dwell among us my imagination raced, much excited, to guess at its use, and when I saw what it was for I was filled with great admiration for the orderly way our girls are taught to garden. The lassie took the rod and laid it on the firm fine soil, pressing it in, and repeated the act at regular intervals all down the frame, till lo! the tracks shone fair and clear wherein we were to cradle our babes. Neat straight grooves, marvellously different from the wobbly lines I had been wont, in my despicable ignorance, to draw with a clumsy ardent finger in the old days.

The magical moment of planting had come, and we sat on the milking stool, near by, to open the packets of seeds; lingering luxuriously over the sweetness of their promise, and chattering about the funny habits of plants.

The lassie's packet of foxglove seeds poured into her hand in a slender stream of golden-brown, fine as sand, but my hollyhock seeds were exactly like tiny oysters; like little "natives" before they are opened, as one sees them piled in tubs at Driver's when the months have an "r" in their names. I learned, in our luminous chat, a most unfortunate secret about the domestic life of cucumbers. She was telling me of the weary hours spent at her college in picking off the gentlemen blooms, for marriage, it seems, embitters cucumbers.

"If ever you get a bitter cucumber she is a married lady," quoth the maid.

Which interested me very much.

The western wind took on a sultry crackling quality, making us glance apprehensively at a thundery bank of cloud where the sun was going to bed, and we left our playing to hurry back to work. We had to deepen the bamboo lines a little for my natives, and then I was set to place each one separately two inches apart while she dribbled her finicky foxglove children with great patience down the long shallow lines at the other end of the frame.

"You can never sow seeds too thinly," she

preached, patting a fine blanket of soil over the tiny creatures, and I mused mournfully on the lavish abandon of our sowings in the ignorant years gone by.

Tatty-Bogle, who was sitting on the frame squinting at us with besotted admiration, suddenly received a bang on the head from the first menacing bullet of the thunderstorm; he shot off for the house with stark astonishment in his tail. We drew the glass roof of the frame over our cradled nurslings, put away our tools, and hurriedly followed him.

CHAPTER X

THE FORTUNE-TELLER

. . . Flutter on little worlds, that float in the ether of space !
Flutter on little hearts, whom the great Heart feeds and encloses. . . .
EDWARD CARPENTER.

TWO things happened one mild Christmas which prevented anybody regretting the unseasonable warmth ; the yellow jasmin by the front door burst out into a sheet of golden bloom, and the stylosa irises under the terrace gave us a generous heaped-up offering of their exquisite fragrant flowers of lilac and blue. The flowers that bloom when most flowers are dead are, I often think, the most dearly loved of all ; and we lingered, enchanted beside our treasures feeling very rich because of them.

It was a memorable Christmas for other reasons too, the house-party cooked its own dinner and the mathematician taught us how to tell fortunes in a new and very exciting way.

Nowadays we look back on the many servants of pre-war days without any regret, but at first the shortage of domestic labour pressed heavily not in mine alone, but also in countless other British homes; we had always had cheap and plentiful labour in these isles; the leisured women were quite untrained and unprepared for housework, unlike Canada, Australia and the United States, where the problem has been faced from the first with sound common sense.

As soon as her war-baby was adopted my last indoor domestic dashed off to "munitions," leaving me only my loyal friend the gardener, who was too old to enlist. A period of distressful overwork followed, during which I learned with increasing enlightenment, however, what an imposition petted servants had become, and faced the new burden of housework added to the daily tale of war-work in an office up in London, with actual mental, if not physical, relief.

But the baptism was fierce at first. I had not an idea of anything—I could not boil a potato, and the horrors of cabbage cooked without salt or soda made me hate the very sight of greens for months. Cleaning was comparatively easy. I had learned much in hospital days, but even that, I found, had its special household skeins of mystery. The aluminium pots could not be cleaned with soda, and silver abhorred brass polish. But those were minor magics beside the tortuous entanglements of cooking.

I stumbled among the bewildering chemistries of

heat and cold, of salt and sweets, of food values complicated to a labyrinthine puzzle in those difficult days by the whims and moods of the Food Controller and the ever-present factor of divergent palates in the family circle. I made stubborn failure after failure till the gardener with pitiful understanding arrived one day from his home with a bright-featured, sensible, laughing woman:

" I've brought the wife to help you, Ma'am ":—and with her assistance I at last got the daily routine systematised and life simplified down to its finest edge. For I knew, as soon as I found myself toiled up with endless dish-washing, sink-scouring, and so on, that the first need was to eliminate every unnecessary body-comfort in order to find leisure for the treasured comfort of the mind. Breakfast retained its ancient splendour; there could be no meanness about the first meal of the day; but luncheon vanished, an unnecessary indulgence, superseded by tea at 3 o'clock and followed by dinner at eight.

As I got the daily routine running smoothly like a hospital schedule, and a thousand readjustments of time were made, I found guests and friends, as well as the household, becoming acclimatised to the new idea of waiting on themselves instead of being waited on; only I had first myself to master the whole principle of housework, and learn how to tell everyone what to do; and when to do it.

I was pleased to find my kingdom house-proud; sound at the core; as each new need came along it was faced with spirit; when we could not get the real thing we went without; but everyone worked good and hearty to get the real thing. No imitation honey; no dyed swedes labelled jam; no margarine rolled into pats and besprigged with parsley to look like butter, ever found favour at our board in the harshest days of short commons.

In spite of the extra trouble entailed upon us all, in our degree, by keeping goats, everyone worked light-heartedly and declared that their new milk and rich pale butter and cheese were well worth the extra trouble. Moreover, we quickly grew to see that in order to get the very best out of life you need the spice of the fun of working for it. It takes brains and grit to win one's comforts for oneself. I suppose that is why the pioneer settler is the pastoral aristocrat; there is no pride like his brave pride.

"After all, what is the use of birth if it cannot serve you at need," said a girl at the sink one morn, soon after I had got the wheel of these new methods revolving. She was a black-haired, grey-eyed siren who practised the old English art of morris dancing; I looked at her tall slender figure swathed in an overall, from where I sat in the kitchen entrenched behind onions, carrots and potatoes, and a tiny atom of meat, the week's allowance from the Food

Controller for the whole household. I knew very well she was not speaking to me, but he of Eton and " the Shop " who stood beside her did not reply, he was polishing the glass and china, as she rinsed them in the warm suds, his arms spinning like a lapidary's wheel ; perhaps he thought what she said needed no answer. It set me thinking, however. Breed and education are good things for women to see to it their children have—a rock to anchor to in time of storm. They are staunch props to lean on in one's friends these days, when the feudal system is giving its last kick in the history of England, and the age of harsh class distinction has begun its difficult passing into the wider brotherhood which our children's children will surely enjoy.

The flowery Christmas with which I started the chapter was the first one at which we had no servant to help, and did all our own work ; and it happened to be the one at which we were presented with the vastest turkey I have ever possessed. A nightmare beast, which hung in the larder to the utmost joy of all beholders but myself ; for I knew full well it had to be drawn and trussed, and these were mysteries beyond my education. I would revolve round the animal miserably regarding it, wondering how I was ever going to get it to look like the turkeys we had carved so many merry Christmas days, till at last there dawned the fateful 24th, when I knew, whatever blunders were committed, the bird must be somehow induced to part with much and be stuffed with more.

At breakfast I heard the mathematician mourning his figure. "There was a time," said he, "when everyone told me how thin I was and now everyone tells me how fat I am. There must have been a time when I crossed the borderland; there must have been a time if it was only half an hour when I was the right size, only no one ever told me of it."

I was so impressed by the exactitude of such a mind that I reflected he might assist me in my own troubles, and later on lured him into the kitchen to pick his brains.

He was a frail reed, for with all his drawings, plans and calculations of weight and diameters he never arrived at the necessary moment of subtraction and addition on the actual body of the bird.

It was the sailor-man who finally saved us both; he conceived the brilliant idea of driving me, turkey and all, down to the poulterer in the town, who not only performed the necessary rites but with true sympathy permitted me to watch his work and learn how the deed was done. Whereupon work among the cook-pots proceeded with great merriment, and the sailor-man became very masterful about the sauces, eclipsing us all with his epicurean guile. He put too much nutmeg in the bread-sauce though.

Our mathematician was considerably mortified, and pondering how he might retrieve our full regard,

THE FORTUNE-TELLER

asked for a large brass bowl, a taper, and some walnut shells. When the early twilight deepened into dark and the curtains were drawn; when the fitful light of a great wood fire glimmered on brass and copper, spinning webs of shadow over oaken chests and settles, sending spurts of light like accusing fingers into the face of the old grandfather clock; when happy tired faces were circled round the red hearth to roast chestnuts and gossip of old times and friends, he yielded up his secret. He set the big brass bowl on an oak chest and offered to tell our fortunes.

He leaped at once into tremendous popularity and we crowded round his oracle. The bowl was three-parts full of water and round the edge were stuck pieces of stamp paper bearing figures. Floating on the water was a tiny boat made of half a walnut shell with the taper standing up like a little mast. The Art Critic, being of solemn aspect, was given a long manuscript and told off to read the words; the taper was lighted and one by one we approached to stir the water and send the wee boat sailing to our fate; being first earnestly warned to avoid swamping it by too much vigour, as that makes an irretrievable warning of sudden death.

With blanched visage the morris dancer approached and stirred delicately. The tiny craft moved, circled, and finally swam to number twenty, where it cuddled and rested.

"These are the words of Wisdom told on a steep hill, by fire upon water," chanted the Prophet from his high chair: "A wheaten loaf, a jar of honey, a loving mate for you."

She flushed maidily, and professed bewilderment.

"It's jolly good," said the sailorman bluffly, "the simple life and much happiness. Hope mine's as good," and he set the boat plunging dangerously.

We held our breath till it stayed by number ten and then laughed at his discomfiture to hear that—

"Seven fair sons and seven dark daughters shall rise and call you blessed."

He retired to digest this news with the aid of a glass of port; and one by one the merry crowd went up to the bowl to learn their fortune.

Our tall Diana left the piano where she was singing "John Peel" in a dear, delightful, crakey voice which seemed to give the General's heart a thrill and came up next to sail her barque.

"You fiddle while Rome is burning," said the Oracle,—a fate which she declared was dowdy and indecisive, but which earned her a very direct glance from a pair of soldierly eyes, and made me wonder as she swept back to the piano how much longer her haughty indifference would withstand a determined siege. Their owner followed her to the holly-hung shadows and brought her back to see

THE FORTUNE-TELLER

his fate :—" Our Fate " :—I heard him murmur as they passed under the big mistletoe bough, and smiled in my heart to see her fascinated and reluctant eyes fall at the words.

We crowded round him, for the whole household loved them both and dumbly wished him well. He stirred the water carefully and the boat danced derisively to and fro and round and about, till it wearied and slowed and found his number.

" Thirty-eight," sang out the mathematician, and the Wizard read :

" The first word that is spoken to-morrow will be the keynote of your whole future." Diana fled back to " John Peel " and I registered a vow that I would hiss " yes " through his keyhole at break of day.

My gardener lassie sat apart, watching the two with dewy thoughtful eyes ; presently she slipped upstairs and missed the Fortune Designer's own fortune which told him that " childless and forlorn you deserve your fate " rousing the sailor-man to unholy mirth.

The door opened and in came the girl with a bunch of tabby fur in her arms whence glowed a pair of green astonished eyes.

" He is going to try our lonely soldier's fortune," she said.

We had toasted the American at dinner, and wondered how he fared in France, and if he thought of us in the Surrey garden. The maiden's notion pleased us much and we set the petted cat beside the bowl, where he promptly bent his head and lapped up a long drink; when we tried to make him stir the water he shook his paw, mewed noisily, and started to lick it. We pleaded with him, reasoned, and begged, but he was fatuously content to purr and watch us, till the lass gave up and tried her own fate.

"A brave man will bring home the V.C. to you," said the Prophet. She paled, gazing down with a still inward glance which made the gunner catch his breath.

"Scalps, my dear, scalps!" said the big playwright, advancing violently to the fray. He was pushing back his cuff to make a deep long stir when the puss-cat saw the swaying boat and sat tensely up to regard it, as though he had not been asked to do so a dozen times already.

"Hullo! What's that?" he seemed to say, patting the walnut shell gently to and fro and coquetting gingerly with this new kind of mouse. Presently the lighted taper came too near his nose and he jumped off the table in a rage, leaving us excitedly watching the American's fate:—the small ship bobbed and ploughed a way to number fourteen and our mystery merchant read the riddle.

"You build a sunlit future, with long shadows."

"Why shadows?" queried the Mathematician.

THE FORTUNE-TELLER

"Long shadows mean long life, they come at sunset," said one, gleefully patting her cat.

The game proceeded apace; and the playwright was much thrilled to learn he must "hoe the hard row to-day, for to-morrow waits rich harvest."

When the punch bowl was brought in we all gathered round for the last ritual of the day; the thin wooden ladle, silver bound, with a long handle of twisted whalebone was solemnly handed to me by the "Chief Guest" to do its yearly office. We crowned the exact-minded man who had taught us our new game with a gaudy cracker cap and named him Chief Guest as sign of our forgiveness and approval, and after sipping the warm cordial we all joined hands to sing our lusty "Auld Lang Syne."

I love that song. Life seems good to me every year afresh when I look on long-loved faces, and hear the same words ring round the board where care has been dropped for a brief day or two, and love and friendship reign supreme.

"Frae morning sun till dine" pealed out, and just then I heard the grandfather clock clear his old throat to strike midnight. An electric thought shot through my heart, I felt the hand each side of mine tighten suddenly as if the same thought had darted into two other brains, and on the General's face a tense frown deepened. Before the clock had droned its message out the sailor broke into our song with a mighty shout:

"Have we all had a happy Christmas?"

The last stroke of midnight died and the morrow dawned on a laughing, cheering, unanimous "Yes."

Diana turned to her man with a sweetness of surrender that sent the rest of us tip-toeing happily upstairs.

.   .   .   .   .

We have played the game many times since, and in case any reader cares to try it too, here is the Mathematician's list of "fates"; but of course it is easy to write any number of fresh ones to suit oneself. It makes a very appropriate and amusing game for a New Year party.

THE WISDOM WORDS AS TOLD BY FIRE UPON WATER, FOR YOU.

1. A long road to a welcoming hearth, where waits a warm mate and true.
2. Where other folk's hens lay one egg yours shall lay two; your reapers shall grasp a full sheaf.
3. You, for your giving the more will you get, for trusting your fellows leave friends round your sons.
4. You will win a lover brilliant as dawn: fierce as Typhoon: strong as death.

THE FORTUNE-TELLER

5. Health without effort: wealth without work: happiness without hypocrisy.
6. You will surprise your friends before this year is out.
7. You fiddle while Rome is burning.
8. A brave man will bring home the V.C. to you.
9. Your hands are clever if your tongue is slow; they will carve riches from strange stones.
10. Seven fair sons and seven dark daughters shall rise and call you blessed.
11. Desired of many, you shall yet lose the most desired.
12. The trap is set with a golden bait.
13. You sleep, and you dream—and your dreams come true.
14. You build a sunlit future with long shadows.
15. You will tread in the mart of Gods, and be paid in the currency of Immortals.
16. Peace and honour and a famous grave.
17. The true mate for you is a little boat.
18. Riches with content; silence with admiration; gladness without regret.
19. Your pen is your shield and buckler.
20. A wheaten loaf, a jar of honey, a loving mate for you.
21. Where you pass men will smile; and women weep.
22. Hoe the hard row to-day, for to-morrow waits rich harvest,

THE GARDEN OF EXPERIENCE

23. You will find a gold mine where you least expect it.
24. Shells without kernels, a hearth without a flame, hope without its fruit.
25. A dark-haired mortal is enamoured of you.
26. You are treading on thin ice.
27. Your fate awaits you at a far port.
28. You would do well to be kind as you are strong.
29. Roses, roses all the way and at the end a meeting.
30. Beware of your powerful fascination, it wrecks as well as it builds.
31. That episode in your past is known to one who plans vengeance.
32. You are too fond of money. Forget it.
33. You have never yet been fully appreciated; in the coming year you will.
34. Let nothing tempt you from the path of great romance.
35. You will take every turn of fortune with a high heart.
36. Beware, you who go so gaily down the flowery path of dalliance; there are snakes within the grass.
37. Leave behind the chilly North, and the sunny South will fill your life with radiance.
38. The first word that is spoken to you to-morrow will be the keynote of your whole future.

THE FORTUNE-TELLER

39. You will shortly meet a beloved friend, whom you have not seen for years.
40. You should settle in the land to which your next sea-voyage takes you; for in it fame and fortune wait.
41. Do not let your enemy intimidate you; for his downfall will be swift and sure.
42. Green eyes have not dogged you for nothing :— jealousy dominates your life.
43. A long walk on the rough : a short while on the smooth ; then a loss ; and after that riches and long days.
44. There is negation for you everywhere, because you fear.
45. You do not know what you miss, because you have not wit to want it.
46. More wealth than love ; more clothes than flesh ; more fame than peace.
47. There is need for discretion in your ventures : though there is more success than you deserve.
48. You will become a tamer of wild animals.
49. Childless and forlorn you deserve your fate.
50. Long travel in many lands ; much love at many hands.
51. A brilliant marriage ; a little love ; a lot of praise.
52. Gladness trims both sides the road you face.
53. Silver Foxes will be your mascot.

THE GARDEN OF EXPERIENCE

54. Whatever you shall ask at the fairies' hands next Midsummer Eve shall be yours.
55. You have power to desire, greater than power to keep.
56. Ask: and it shall be given to you.
57. A long road for travelling with a star to guide.
58. Nor has any here the courage to read your fate.
59. Cleverer than kind you have many lovers.
60. Your way is the way you wish; and leads to the waters of Lethe.
61. Sorrow will deepen, not break, the pride of your soul.
62. A wild wind, a wide sky, a win-out trail for you.
63. You will lose lightly: and seek again with tears.
64. Your face is your fortune, and God defend you.
65. They welcome you most, who love you least.
66. Your wit is bitter but your heart is sweet.
67. Gold for you in plenty and the envy of men.
68. You will find content among the blue-gum and wattle; the wallaby and waratah.
69. Remember Solomon!
70. Children will love you all your life.
71. You will win the Calcutta sweep.
72. You will turn your face to the stars and follow a trackless path.
73. They who knock at your door will not turn empty away.
74. You have too many friends to be successful.
75. Hail! Well-beloved . . . !

THE FORTUNE-TELLER

76. Anointed and crowned in the Temple of Fame.
77. To-morrows are your interest; and yesterdays your capital.
78. When you learn to grasp the nettle you will win to joy.
79. There waits for you a long low house, flocks and herds and sunny days.
80. When you see Kauri gum consider it seriously.
81. You have trodden your baser self under foot.
82. The loss of a relative.
83. Marriage will be frustrated by your own imprudence, but that will improve rather than shadow your success in life.
84. You will have no difficulty in winning her but you will find it hard to lose her.
85. Do not let your beauty eclipse your intellect or your intellect your beauty.
86. Your journeyings end in Africa.
87. You are bound and hoodwinked.
88. Middle-age will bring you your greatest romance.
89. A ranch in the Rocky Mountains; a river to fish and game for your gun.
90. A spinning-wheel will sing a golden song to you.
91. A fair wind and a following sea.
92. The fairies attend your birth and you have the high gifts of a poet.
93. Martyrdom in a great cause.
94. Age cannot wither, nor custom stale, your charm.

95. You possess an unsuspected well of inspiration.
96. Yours is the heart in search of experience.
97. Strenuous and deserving you will earn a splendid fate.
98. Breasting the dawn you will taste strife; facing the sunset your will find love; and in the night you will sleep content.
99. There is an inheritance to fall in quickly.
100. A country estate after a competence has been secured.

CHAPTER XI

ROSES

> The woodbine spices are wafted abroad,
> And the musk of the rose is blown. . . .
> TENNYSON.

ONE of the things I have learned in my Garden of Experience has been to let Cupid go free. Anything more dismal than his sulks, when he is used in any confined or decorative sense, I cannot well imagine—or anything more beautiful when he is given a comfortable place to roam in at his will.

He is a comparatively new and very appealing rose; vigorous of growth when he is happy, with long buds of a deep, flushed, tawny cream—which open out to large semi-double blooms of a most attractive warmth of tone; and he blooms on the old wood.

Beside my front door is a terra-cotta Ali-Baba jar; I like its shape and weather-beaten mellow texture; it was made in the local pottery, and given to me by an old servant, of whom I was very fond. She married an officer during the war, and we have since lost touch. The Ali-Baba jar stands to me for all of simplicity and sincerity. I am very attached to it, remembering the much of giving it stands for, devoted service on the woman's part and ungrudging gratitude on mine. So when, on a day, a friend came to stay among the pines, and presented me with a sturdy little "Cupid" in memory of his visit, to be tended in my garden of friendship, I decided to plant it in the Ali-Baba jar, and reflected how nice it would be when the blooms stretched around my doorway and brushed the lips of those who entered in. But Cupid would none of these fancies. I planted him ceremoniously in the jar, and he resisted the bondage of his environment to the point of death. I tended and served him; but he fretted incessantly; no long arms flung up to the sun and stars, no bloomy buds, no shower of scented colour—hardly, indeed, a show of leaf. After long patience I decided that his artificial home did not suit the beautiful creature, and on a wet and windy day in November, when all the perfumes of autumn trailed reedily across the garden-work, I transplanted Cupid. I took him away from bricks and mortar to an open space unlittered with such man-made paraphernalia; there he grows apace, rioting his wild heart out in a very tempest of bloom. I have now found a homely little white rose, of temperate habits and modest appearance, to fill the Ali-Baba jar; and folks who go in and out of my door in rose-time are greeted with a deep delicious perfume from it. I hardly know of any rose, unless it is the old, old "cabbage" which radiates so strong and sweet a fragrance; it puzzles people I find—they seldom suspect at first the unpretentious blossom at their elbow.

A happy trick with rambler roses will bear describing because I find it very satisfying as the years test out the idea, the only real test; and also I find no one else who has tried it in just my way. In the old days of first experimental ignorance I had a passion for arches covered with roses, but I found, on living with them, that they invaded the vision too much, and dwarfed the garden, and, more important still, the best blooms were always on top of the arches, and therefore out of sight. One day I conceived the idea of cutting the wire arches down, and edging the big path on the lawn with them. The result was a sort of scalloped effect, an avenue of wire festoons which became in time well draped with the rambling roses, and exceedingly pretty. But I made the mistake at first of mixing the colours and varieties; a great mistake, and one it has taken time to recover. Beginners nearly always fear to plant in masses of one variety, and yet that is the only way to get bold and satisfying effects. Everyone who walks down the garden path now, flanked with its low arches of rambling roses, can look down on sheets of bloom, and admire the undulating decoration of half circles outlined in roses. One of the advantages of this half-arch scheme is that the wire is so completely covered. It is distressful to see, in the orthodox arch, a long leggy, wiry space a yard or so from the ground up on either side, covered with only a few leafless spindles of stem, and then for the rest of the erection a bower of bloom on top, high above one's head. It gives a top-heavy effect, like a fat woman in a tight skirt with tiny feet. To anyone who has a sentiment for passing under rose arches the idea will be anathema, because the only way of traversing to and fro beneath my variety would be on all fours. But personally I have outgrown the leaning to that form of romance, for I found, by living on intimate terms with rose arches, that they scratch one's face a great deal; and, indeed, I have heard some fateful language from friends on dark nights as they turned from the glowing open door of farewells into the dark rose-bowered path towards the garden gate, and met long thorny sprays in the face. The wind always takes good care that all the tying in the world will not save you from loose sprays.

In my Garden of Ignorance I used to make a very great mistake at first among the rambling roses. I was mean about pruning. I got close-fisted and hated to part with the old wood. I could not trust the amazing vigour of the roots to fling up fresh leaders year after year, and I played

"To-night is the night of the dead." *Chap. XVII.*

around in a lady-like manner with a pruning knife, behaving as though I had met a group of tea roses in need of attention. And so, of course, the bloom grew spare and sulky, and the abundance of succulent green crowned with great heads of lusty bloom which I saw in other people's gardens never came my way at all. I complained bitterly, and was warned by wise-acres about my mistakes, but somehow autumn after autumn I dallied and minced among the old wood, unable to trust.

One day a friend put a powerful pair of sécateurs in my hand for a birthday gift, remarking that all that rubbish in the roses wanted something stronger than my little knife. The size and strength of the instrument went to my head, I believe, for I passed to the nearest Dorothy Perkins and shore every strand to the ground, shutting my eyes as I did it, and gave up the rose for lost. The harsh treatment gave the rambler the exact fillip it needed; next spring it was a maze of strong green, and in July bore excellent shoots. So I learned my lesson. And now every December, when the last beloved bud has bowed to frost, I go round and cut with ruthless vigour. In a more reasonable frame of mind, truly, for I do not now shave the whole structure of the ramblers to the ground, but cut out every bit of wood that has bloomed, leaving only the lusty young virgin shoots to bloom next season, and of those I leave the strongest and the best. The ramblers are immensely grateful for manure water through May and June, and amply repay the trouble such fare involves.

Some of the pale ramblers, like Goldfinch, have a very warm intimate perfume, and help considerably to furnish one's garden with the attributes of beauty, of which most certainly fragrance is one. A variety very little known but most beautiful is Robert Craig. It opens with a deep orange-yellow bud of good substance, very like William Allen Richardson in colour, and as it opens it pales, arriving by beautiful gradations to a creamy pink, and finally to a full globular rose of dead white, heavy, with a very luscious scent which friends variously describe as like very strong sweetbrier or else like pineapple. This rose never mildews, grows very vigorously, and has beautiful glossy foliage, with brown shoots in the early stages. I can never understand why it is not in every garden; nor ever cease to be glad that I have had the good fortune to grow it in mine; I saw it first in Bide's nursery garden, and have always rejoiced that Robert and I met!

The word " rose " conjures up a veritable picture gallery of happy memories . . . from the initial moment of digging the hole, which is to be filled with a toothsome compound of clay, loam, basic slag and decayed manure, for the rapacious young rose tree awaiting planting (roses are very greedy guests, with abominable table manners) to the ultimate glowing perfumed day when we sit on the lawn sorting damask petals for pot-pourri.

In my garden with its thin soil, the extreme of attention, not to say petting and spoiling, has been devoted to the cultivation of roses. Black currants, onions, sweet peas, pansies and such gormandisers I have frankly avoided as being beyond our means to satisfy in this sandy valley; but for roses there could be no nay. Laboriously, and from afar, year after year, manure and loam have been hauled up the steep sandy lane which gives access to this habitation; these necessities entail a good deal of expense, and therefore I have ruthlessly forgone most "heavy doers" for the sake of the roses we dearly love. One year came in the nature of a rose festival; the flagged garden which was given up to beans, carrots and other useful but homely products during the pinch of war, was able to be reinstated under the rule of its former dynasty. No more loyal subjects ever welcomed back the reign of the roses.

The beds to which they returned had been so soundly rested and reinforced by the nitrates formed by the leguminous peas and beans, that the ritual of planting was considerably curtailed.

At the very bottom of the rose garden runs a hedge of that boisterous grower, American Pillar, sandwiched in alternate plantings by the coy

Aviateur Blériot; on the flagged spaces are laid out four oblong beds, with a great centre circle divided into four more beds. Obviously these last must be planted with one variety, in order to satisfy a sense of design. After long and anguished consultation with a score of catalogues we decided on General MacArthur. There were several reasons for this choice; one is that the cold grey stone of the flagged garden seems to need a warm deep colour in the centre, framed as it is by the blues of wistaria, anchusa, iris, nepeta, etc., in the herbaceous beds on the terrace above. Other good reasons for the choice of General MacArthur are: its heavy perfume, its shapely growth, the fine carriage of its blooms on long stalks; and its great good heart for blooming in the autumn.

We have learned how to use Lady Hillingdon indoors. All round the brown panelled study at eye-level runs a bookshelf, and on top of it silver vases of this orange rose fulfil a beautiful mission. Taking a book out in rose-time is quite definitely associated nowadays with looking up into the blooms of that beauty. Most of us who have tried to use Lady Hillingdon in table decoration find how her thin weak stem lets the bloom hang down.

The bed that ranges alongside of this yellow one is fraught with excitement, inasmuch as it is to be devoted to a dozen plants of that much praised American rose, "Los Angelos." I am told that it combines the best points of Madame Abel Chatenay and Lyon, with the faults of neither. Excited anticipation, therefore, runs high. In the far opposite corner is a stalwart bed of Snow Queen (*née* Frau Carl Druschki), whose wonderful white blossoms make a glory of the twilight. Long experience of this robust and gratifying creature has persuaded me that her only faults are lack of perfume and a truly desperate need of disbudding.

In another bed is a rose which I know is full of faults, but for which we cherish an obstinate affection, Mrs. Longworth, to wit, whose petals striped rose and cream, with their outward waxen sheen and inward velvet texture, have bred in us a loyal devotion which none of her faults can corrupt. Mrs. Longworth needs persistent disbudding, is inclined to ball, and has a briary habit of growth. But we love her.

Away in odd corners will go such beloved troubadours as Mrs. Massey, Ideal, Betty, and Irish Elegance. I heard there was a horse running of that name in a certain famous race one year, and deposited an adventurous sovereign thereupon, because I admire the rose, to the sevenfold improvement of my exchequer.

The nurseryman who plies his attractive trade near the town which our village fringes, has a rose-foreman who is a most enticing fellow. He looks kind and fatherly, benevolent and guileless; it is only after one has trodden the long rough fields with him and heard his seductive chatter about each new rose that one realises he is a snake in the garden and that we are in our own listening hearts the eternal and temptable Eve.

One windy day, late in the year, the lass-I-love and I decided we would like a long walk. Accompanied by Dandy, who heartily prefers the hedgerows to my study, we started out blithely to sniff the sweet saddened autumnal winds. Aimlessly plodding along I told her a story of the Battery Hill at Rye, where I had sat one night many years ago and listened to the lorn cry of plovers rising up through the low-lying mist on the salt marshes below the town ; I told her the story in one of those absorbed moments when the barriers of age and a common sex are swept away between mother and daughter, and all is clear and strong between them in the dazzling honesty of an indestructible sweet love. Of how my life had reached a tragic hour, and that forlorn note gave me great courage to live on—for the cry of plovers, they say, is the mourning of the souls of childless women and they could not hurt me because I held under my heart the sweet and absolute assurance of her life—the promise of her coming.

As we talked our feet turned (bidden by that insistent, unregarded, but so potent sense, the subconscious mind) toward the Alma Nurseries, for the way leads across wide rolling fields where plovers build their guarded nests and cry the mother cry every spring of the year. Far away over a hill Bide's tended acres broke into view, and at that sight we quickened our steps.

"Let's go and see what new roses he has," said we, and raced merrily down into the very net of the subtle wiles of the rose-foreman.

He led us, unresisting, willing slaves, to his rose-acres where stubby bits of wood peered above the clodded soil, looking at us with hardy self-assurance —they the muddied tramps gazed up into our lofty faces with unwinking pride, full sure that soon we should be humbly begging to buy them for the bloom-sweetness hidden under their rags and tatters.

"This," said our kind old Serpent, "is the Queen Alexandra rose, an improved Juliet, with a fine upright stem and handsome foliage. She has all the bizarre colour which made Juliet famous."

We eyed the spindly spikes labelled "The Queen Alexandra Rose," picturing the wild gipsy habits of the baggage Juliet corrected, her unrestrained tendencies allayed by cooling infusions of nobler blood so that now we can have all of her beauty with the further advantage of good deportment and correct carriage.

"And this," went on the Snake, "is Magnolia; she has a long yellow bud like Sunburst, but opens out wide like a water-lily."

We were becoming hypnotised as usual, and saw in our minds great beds of roses set with wide creamy shallow waxen blooms, golden-hearted as the lilies of the lake.

"And this," relentlessly, "is Titania, a copper-coloured noisette, rambling in growth; beautiful but not erect."

A vision straightway flushed our minds of the weak-kneed lady, sprawling all over the place without any attempt at decent manners; blooming freely enough, in a dissolute wandering way, and earning the love of growers for her silken petals of copper salmon and yellow. Presently we heard that a cousin of hers and Juliet's is the new hybrid Austrian Copper Briar, named President Bouche—being assured that though he is a free fellow, thorny of growth, he reveals a tender heart of soft coral-red, shading to prawn.

Anon he led us to Red Letter Day, and before those stark spikes we fell heavily, for we had already seen a bloom or two of that new semi-double scarlet-crimson rose, and knew that it both grows very freely out of doors and shines indoors with a very brilliant ray; it is as invaluable an addition to the repertoire of red roses as Commander Jules Gravereaux, the "poppy-rose," which has lived unchallenged in our love since he was launched on a troubled world years ago, the child of Frau Karl Druschki and Captain Hayward, with the colour and sweet scent of his father and the golden heart of his mother.

Anon we took our way across the plover-haunted fields, much encumbered but also much elated, with a large bundle of the newest roses; the while I learned a long sad story of the frightful faults of the rose-beetle. With a grave distaste for doing it I have entertained suspicions of his activities for many and many a moon. Perhaps others, misled as I by his exceeding beauty, have failed to chase him with the same austerity as the ugly wireworm and others. But it is a weakness, and one we must guard against. I have often—I admit it—watched the charming scarab in his shining cuirass of burnished green and coppery red, admiring, if lamenting, the neat round hole he nibbles in the petals of beloved roses. But now the truth was out and he stood accused of attacking strawberry blossoms in May or June; also peonies, mountain ash, elder, candytuft and the flower of seeding turnips. The grub is a large dirty white one, quite unengaging, like most grubs, and makes very good food for fowls if they are turned out in newly dug soil.

It was with relief I learned the creature had even this small use in our economy.

CHAPTER XII

THE WOOING OF TATTY-BOGLE

Should a creature succeed in maintaining its little profound and complicated existence without overstepping the boundaries of instinct, without doing anything but what is ordinary, that would be very interesting, and very extraordinary.

MAETERLINCK.

I CAN never make up my mind if the great Oriental poppies really move at sunset or if it is their dazzling scarlet which makes my eyes jump. I have watched them often, after a long hot day when the breathless noon has become still twilight, when never a gasp of air stirs a petal, and the frogs are drumming overtures for the nightingales to sing. The poppies stand up stiff on their long, grey, hairy stems, bearing crumpled silk flowers of a scarlet so challenging that it is like the blare of a trumpet ; as the eye dwells upon them they move to a ghostly syncopated rhythm, in the breathless motionless air. I am aware of the snares of an imagination which can see anything, once it gets going. So I have sat with others of an evening and watched the poppies do their uncanny dance. It's all the sleep they are heavy with that nods their heads, perhaps, but whatever it is, the other people see it as well as I. And the bed of mixed colours, the salmon pink and deep maroon, the crushed strawberry and pale pink Oriental poppies dance too, as well as the scarlet ones ; though I am bound to say that their movement seems even more unreal and elusive. I cannot help believing the quivering colour has a great deal to do with it.

Talking of colour, how little the town-dusty eye sees in a garden at first ; one of the real pleasures of entertaining has been to watch that awakening to the secret beauties of the valley as city senses become quickened and attuned ; ears, dulled by traffic roar and screech, lose by degrees in the garden their coarseness of apprehension, and learn to know and listen for the faintest, frailest gossamer sounds of song ; become in time, indeed, so keen that they can hear the tiny scurrying sounds of happy mating life in the undergrowth of the woods at night. Eyes, dimmed by glare of brick and mortar, inflamed by late nights and electric light, lose their strain in cool deep glades of green. Puckered brows and peering eyes go back to town from the garden-life, full-glanced and open-browed, well-washed by moonlight and by starlight, and the dew bath of the dawn.

They turn to the obvious things at first, but after that progress is rapid, mostly dependent on the individual intelligence. I am always happy to hear the first word of awakening:

"What a wonderful colour there is in that border!" delivered with the air of a Columbus, and generally directed, I find, to the groupings of bizarre tulips and cheiranthus Pamela Purshouse. And then, by and by, more chatter: "I wonder if you have noticed how well that bed of snapdragons and blue stuff blend!" and I gravely wonder with them, refraining from tales of the long, long effort to grow that rose-pink variety or the dastardly winters which freeze out the catmint, and leave us, some summers, with our stock of "blue stuff" shorn to a fragment . . . that lovely shimmering grey-blue like the mist on a river at sundown, which riots in the sandy soil and which the bees love.

They gossip at first in the new-found world of wonder, these dear city-scorched friends, but by and by the full splendour breaks, and they bathe, silenced, in deep wells of vision. I see the harassed faces turn to look at tossed tassels of the larch, the russet of pine-buds, and, later, the pale bloom of the dust of their pollen; see them begin to notice the young satin of the beeches and the lace of silver birch; till a worshipping peace heals the world-worry in their hearts, and the spell of the garden smoothes their loved faces with its own peculiar beauty.

With those few who come fore-armed in a

THE WOOING OF TATTY-BOGLE 245

gardener's knowledge I pass pleasant hours of sophisticated converse, where the subtler moments of garden effort have expressed themselves; they stop at a place where a bush, whose name I have forgotten, mingles its plumes like pink laburnum with pale rose columbines and a trail of purple clematis; they linger, too, by the long border where Love o' Jove is edged with thrift and backed by iris, Queen of May, and purple herbaceous lupins; and are always arrested by the autumn tangle of Tritomas and Michaelmas daisies.

Some particular souls make their own little pet shrine of admiration, and focus much joy in a small space. One friend in the last few years has guarded a guilty love in his bosom because he could not restrain his affection for a certain rose bush which grows a tawny blossom shaped like a wild rose, with a golden back to its petals, and a deep, fiery-flame face . . . and he learned in a painful hour that it was the Austrian Copper Briar rose. Of enemy origin.

Another friend would always sit on the mound above the terrace and look down to the tulips from a point where pines dominate the scene, finding so much of pleasure there that she must needs lure another guest to share it with her, a companionship of admiration which led me ultimately and in due course to the expense of a silver christening mug; not an infrequent result of sojourn in the Garden of

Experience, by the way, as many homes in this England Isle may testify.

Even the baby girl, "little heart-o'-gold," before she grew up into a learned gardener, with diploma and all complete, found her own pet spot to stand and garner beauty, considering with wide child-eyes the antics of a magenta bounder called Cranesbill, who would riot in the rock garden, do what I might to try and keep him quiet, and give his more refined companions a chance; a lusty gaudy fellow, whose overpowering colour made her slim young freshness look like a light moth blown in the wind, as she stood regarding him.

There is no knowing what people will turn into after they have lived in the garden for a while. Sometimes I feel as if it has a magic, because guests change so quickly and so completely into entirely different people from the ones they pretend they are and bring down and present to us on first acquaintance with the place. Perhaps it is a Circe-spot, where none may escape a spell. There was that admirer of Tatty-Bogle, I remember; his was a most astounding change. During an artistic "crush" one day in London this man intimated to me that he would appreciate and accept an invitation to the Garden of Experience. Now, although I am bond slave to my garden plot and was much flattered by his hint, I hesitated to proffer an invitation.

"It's just a little sandy pitch in Surrey," I

argued; "happy, but very simple; there is nothing grand about it at all."

He had written a very remarkable and successful play, then in full blast; was being fêted by the proudest hostesses; was always extravagantly dressed and flaunted a rather flamboyant "strong man" type of good looks. I much admired his play, and was mildly interested in his queer personality, but he was the very last person in London to whom I would have dreamed of offering the freedom of my garden. What had this exotic of the theatre to do with a wee little flower patch in our English countryside? He seemed a bit hurt.

"On your own head be it," I protested; and down he came.

I remember it so well. I was bedding out petunias when the rumble of the cab got me up, unwilling, from my knees, to meet him at the garden gate; he was glorious in fine raiment and mountains of luggage, the Lion of the London season, looking awfully out of place at my cottage door; I gave him my wrist to shake as my hands were covered with soil.

I made the usual initial effort at being a good hostess, and ended up by doing exactly what I always do, which is whatever I want to do every day, and leaving him to do the same, with the usual result. He slipped into a rut of effortless charm which endeared him to the whole household, and he finally crystallised into an object of devoted hero-worship, as he was discovered to have been, in his youth, amateur champion boxer of the Pacific coast.

By degrees I began to suspect him of a jealously hidden innermost self; of a heart-core as unlike his world-mask as it is possible to conceive, and it was the Tatty-Bogle who put me on the scent.

I can readily understand anyone admiring the Tatty, but this man did more than admire, he devoured his every movement with an earnest devotion that had behind it the spark of real animal passion. And once when the cat hurt his leg our friend scoured the countryside for unguents, bandages and like courtesies, which were quite useless, as Tatty scornfully looked after his own wound and would not be coddled.

Meanwhile the cat, as usual, invested the garden with beautiful pictures: Tatty among the Anchusa, his deep blue eyes gleaming a saucy challenge from a bower of blue; Tatty in the flagged garden mincing daintily from bed to bed and smelling his favourite flowers; he sits on his hind legs and pulls a bloom down with his front paws if it is too high to reach; Tatty coquetting with the bees, whom he thoroughly understands and respects; Tatty in the moonlight looking like a streak of moonlight himself, with his pale cream body and deep shadowed points. Truly enough to engage anybody's admiration, but for this new guest, artist and beauty-lover, he appeared to make a very ecstasy.

I do not know much about myself. It is too much bother to sit still amid the whirling days and try to analyse this queer, crabbed, self-willed complication known as me, with which my unfortunate generation-mates have to jog along the life-road as best they may; but one thing I have come to recognise as a characteristic I must surely reckon with. If anyone lets me know they want anything very much I try hard to help them get it. It's a most unfortunate trait; puts me to a lot of trouble, and generally turns good friends into acid critics, for it is not the having but the wanting which makes people happy, and in spite of knowing that from observation and experience, I invariably hurry around to still the clamour directly anyone raises the wail of want. Like stuffing sweets into children's mouths, I suppose . . . to keep them quiet. My beloved intimate the Tatty-Bogle, who being a Royal Siamese cat is therefore devoted only to one person, began to show me a harassed eye. The playwright pursued him with unwelcome attentions; meat at odd times, kind pats, pleasant snoogly murmurings, all of which were stoutly resisted; but at last the seducer of plighted affections, having been mixed up with the theatre and knowing something of the art of mimicry, took to copying my whistle and my voice, which put Tatty out very dreadfully. He would run, purring, with uplifted tail and little anxious mews to know what I wanted, and stop disgustedly when he arrived at the place of call to find the brilliant eye of a deceiver, with a fresh-shot bird for a bait to endear himself. He was so persistent in his efforts that I became interested, putting all my money on the Tatty-Bogle, for these Siamese cats are the most faithful lovers of one person that I have ever known in the world of cats. One night my distinguished guest caught Tatty and put him in his own bedroom, amply garnished with milk, fish and a very elegantly prepared basket, but after a spitting, snarling couple of hours he let him out and Tatty arrived panting and much disgruntled, with a bushy tail, at his proper place—the foot of my bed. At breakfast the beaten one disgorged his want.

"I wish I had a cat like that," he said, "he's a gem. Loyal as a dog!" I had grown fond of the silly man by this time and immediately fell into my pet snare.

"Would you like me to give you one?" I said. And lo, I loosed once more, as so often, upon myself an avalanche of excitement. He hurried up to town, tidied up matters, and came back for a long visit to write a new play and get his cat.

"A lady cat, please, so that I can have lots of little Tatty-Bogles!"

In my ungovernable amiability I went and sought out my cat to consult him about this possible newcomer, but before I could say a word Tatty-Bogle jumped up on my knee and squinted horribly toward high heaven. The intense sapphire-blue of his eye was nearly drowned in swimming black; I knew there must be an enemy about, for when his pupils grow as big as that he is very frightened. Presently Dandy, the Yorkshire terrier, dashed round the corner in a fearful temper, his little white teeth grinning, and his tail stark with rage. When he saw where Tatty had got to, he gave a disgusted yelp and abandoned the chase; returning, much hurt by his adversary's mean sanctuary, to the corner of the wood which he cherished most—his privy charnel house of smelly bones. I suppose Tatty had committed the indiscretion of walking past it, and roused the food-hog's wrath.

I patted the cat's satin coat, soft coloured as cream, and presently a pair of affronted ears lying flat to the small dark head pricked up again, the dilated pupils narrowed to black slits, and a great deep purr broke from his contented frame. Anon a dark brown paw began to stroke my chin and a hot rough little tongue to lick my neck. Lazily I accepted his endearments wondering how much truth there might be in the stories the occultists tell of these, the Royal Siamese cats, kept by the Buddhist priests with such care in the palaces of the kings of Siam. They call them sacred vehicles for the transmission of royal souls; and those who meddle in matters of the spirit world say that, if a Siamese cat attaches itself to any one person with the passionate devotion, which no other kind of cat gives like the Siamese, that person is immortal ; . . . that is to say, carries a soul which has already passed through a Siamese cat incarnation and is progressing upwards. They say that the little animal, carrying the soul of a migrating human within it, recognises and is kin to the soul which the human shell-case covers. Also they say that many people have no soul at all, only appetites ; and that anyone a Siamese persistently or actively dislikes is soulless.

I stroked Tatty-Bogle's caressing paw as it travelled, tender as thought, up and down on my cheek. If he did indeed carry a soul the human form of it had been, or would be a great lover, I felt sure of that. The high matters of the occultists are something beyond my understanding ; I do not meddle therein. But some people believe in and practise black arts ; there was that old lady I knew, who wanted a Siamese kitten for a pet, remarking with a good deal of firmness to the breeder from whom she bought him that she had been handicapped all her life by being a Victorian female, that she meant to know what it was like to be a male in her next incarnation, and to that end meant to purchase, tend, pet, and study a suitable male host to which her spirit might pass as soon as it left its present flesh-case. Then there was that youth, sad and rather lonely, who besought me for a Siamese cat because he believed that the uneasy spirit of his dead mother whom he loved, and whose " crying heart " he felt about him in his empty home, might come to anchor, so to speak, if he kept and loved one of these occult conveyancers. . . .

Tatty-Bogle heaved himself up with a great sigh, put both arms round my neck, and began to talk to me. No one who has not kept a Tatty-Bogle knows how charmingly he can gossip; answering every question and making comments, grumbling, begging, arguing and behaving quite like one of the family. He had a long love-tale to tell me to-day; he snuggled his dark head shyly into my neck, squeezed me tightly with his chocolate paws, and told me over and over again in the tenderest mews, in cooing, melting gentle slurs of sound, how he loved me and how he loved me till one would think so much love must break his heart.

I remembered the "immortal" story, and let my mind run on psychic matters while I stroked and petted and loved him back. "Perhaps I have a soul," thought I, and puffed for a joyful second. Then reason laid a cooling hand upon this fevered pride.

" The little chap is lonely," said she. " You are all he has to love. Try him with a sweetheart. Then if he leaves all others and cleaves only to you, it will be time enough to study Buddhism and all the Isms of Ind."

When reason hits one full between the eyes it is wisest to throw in the sponge and shake hands with her; so, without saying a word to Tatty about the projected gift behold me, soon afterwards, walking home from the station with a lamenting Siamese lady of high degree in a basket; which was presented to the playwright at tea-time with much ceremony.

But it was a sad sight when the two cats were introduced; at the first glimpse of another cat in his home, every single hair on Tatty's frame went bolt upright and his blue eyes rounded into dense black circles. Affrighted by such a welcome the small lady leaped into my lap for protection, and that was a grievous tactical error. Like a streak of summer lightning, the Tatty-Bogle had followed and pushed her viciously off. Never in his life had he seen another cat upon my knee, and the upset to his temper was terrific. He stormed at her, and then at me. He cursed me in piercing squalls of jealous rage, clung to me with claws at fullest length, lashed his tail, and snarled for a couple of hours or more; nothing, nothing, *nothing* should come between him and me, he declared, nothing on earth. He bade me take the trollop away.

Truly he made such a ghastly to-do, and the blue-eyed pretty one was so grievously neglected that I

THE WOOING OF TATTY-BOGLE 255

believe I would have succumbed to his flattery, turned to Buddhism and fancied that I had a soul, but for the playwright's pleading ; he declared that time was all that Tatty needed, and begged me to give them a real chance. He constructed a sumptuous cattery out of an old sheep-dog kennel, with a very fine wired run, where she would lie out in the sun like a panther, along the branch of a tree, watching the haughty fellow stalk by at my heels whenever I went that way. She would fling little tendernesses after him, soft sounds that made his ears twitch, but that was as far as she got toward melting him.

One day her love-lorn ditty reached the ear of a neighbouring Tom-puss. He was a stout fellow, doughty in love as war, so he hastened to the shrine of neglected beauty and on the way his marauding footfall smote plain on the ear of Tatty-Bogle, who was snoozing in the bushes near by. His ears went back in incredulous wrath ; and I realised, watching, the intense prohibitive jealousy of Tatty's emotional life. However much he had chosen to spurn the overtures of that cloistered beauty, no other male on earth was to provoke a beam from her sapphire eye.

He rose, in the deep shadow of the bushes a wild figure of rage, strangely like a jackal, staring out with ears flat, every hair a-bristle, and tail bushed out like a flue-brush. Suddenly his rival appeared in the full sunshine, padding it hardily toward the desired of all eyes. Tatty-Bogle's face altered with demoniac swiftness and he let out a piercing yell. The intruder turned and instantly a battle royal was in progress.

Finally, in an infernal clatter of teeth, claws and and howls, Tatty drove off his enemy, growling like a young thunderstorm, into the uttermost boundary of the wood; and came back still frightfully excited, to utter pæan after pæan of exultation at the foot of my hammock. Presently he opened his eyes, took breath to lick his wounds, and then espied the coquette, whom I had let out of her palace during his absence, smirking at him from the bushes near by.

And then, to the supreme triumph of the playwright, the wooing of Tatty began, and very pretty it was. He would sit and look at her for hours, devouring every whisker on her lovely high-bred face with passionate eyes. He would lick her face with his little rough tongue, and then sit up like a squirrel, boxing her with his paws, as much as to say:

"Turn your face this way, now that way. Is it possible anything living can be so fair?"

I take no shame to say that a pang of real jealousy shot through my human heart to find myself soulless and superseded. He deserted the foot of my bed at night; and stole Dandy's basket, where he would

"Tatty-Bogle let out a piercing yell." *Chap. XIII.*

"He espied the coquette smirking among the bushes." *Chap. XIII.*

"A figure of wrath, strangely like a jackal." *Chap. XIII.*

fidget restlessly if she were late or coy in coming to bed.

One day, when the playwright was away producing a play in the North, I saw Tatty in a corner tearing up newspaper with teeth and claws. He was terribly busy, hadn't a word to say for himself when I spoke to him. A most unusual sign. He took no notice of me at all, working with frenzied industry at his menial job. Tatty was making a nursery.

Mrs. Tatty-Bogle was crying upstairs in a warm corner of the dressing-room, where she had chosen her own Rotunda ; and by and by, as silence supervened and even busy Tatty fell asleep upon his mound of torn papers, I crept in to look. His wife lay peacefully licking and cuddling five blind *white* kittens : snow-white !

Shocked to the marrow bones by this fearful blot on the escutcheon, I went to the study and consulted a text book on cats to find that Siamese kittens are always born white. Tatty might surely hold his head high and walk proudly. Whereat great relief.

I sent a wire to tell of this affair and the playwright hurried South to welcome the new arrivals. There was high commotion in a day or two when Tatty took one of his children downstairs to the study and started to lick it. Mrs. Tatty rushed after the two, retrieved her babe and, with the little white mite bobbing in her mouth at every step, raced back upstairs to the "nursery" . . . in a few minutes Tatty had it down again, and we had a flurried afternoon running up and down stairs to see neither of them dropped the little one in their quarrel.

In due course they began to shower more little Tatties upon the world. They are all about me as I write : queer talkative gossips with their intense blue eyes and unique coats, uncannily understanding, fierce and gentle, brave and shy. But my Tatty is submerged and become a mere family man ; he spits and snarls no longer, only comes at nights once more to the foot of my bed to explain the great weight of his responsibilities, and how he has spent his time catching mice for others. The playwright owner of these lively particles pets his beloved and increasing hordes. "I loved animals all my life ; I havn't had any for years. I can't tell you what a joy these wonderful little fellows are," he mutters, holding tiny atoms of cream and chocolate fur in his great gentle hands.

Being a gardener I feverishly erect catteries and kittenries to keep pace with him ; once in a liverish moment I made bold to hint that both Tatty and I were getting a trifle snowed under with cats, but the dramatist was superb. He drew a picture of me, as the leader of his warm affections into the joys of cat-keeping . . . of my happy pride in finding his first queen, and presiding over the first nursery. A conscience-smitten woman crept from this astonishing presence, guiltily aware that each succeeding generation had stirred her to lessening enthusiasm, until she had reached the perfidious brink of satiety. A horrid way to entertain the preferences of an honoured guest.

I reflected that even if the kittens did destroy the cretonnes, eiderdowns, rugs and leather chairs, break glass and china, and require the whole household to wait on them that my heart should be bigger than these petty annoyances ; and that my sense of hospitality should prevent me from hinting that I had noticed them. It is painful to learn as one tramps along the life-road how selfish one can grow about things one loves. I love my home.

I suppose that when our generation has passed into history some bright soul will write the life-story of Benrimo, playwright-poet, and make no end of a good book out of it, with all the beauty and imagination of *The Yellow Jacket* and *The Willow Tree* for background to the difficult and kaleidoscopic personality which no two people describe alike. But I feel very sure no one will draw him in the peculiar light in which we of the Garden see his features ;— a cat-lover . . . with the eye of a gallant, jaw of a pirate, heart of a visionary, and head of a genius ; an irascible, irresponsible but engaging creature.

CHAPTER XIII

JAM AND THE COOK-POTS

> . . . In . . . linnet-haunted garden-ground
> Let still the esculents abound.
> . . . And I, being provided thus
> Shall with superb asparagus,
> A book, a taper, and a cup
> Of country wine, divinely sup.
>
> R. L. STEVENSON.

SINCE the upheaval of war we have learned to pursue all our pleasant home-crafts ourselves, without the aid of servants. The garden has become a new wonderland; we gather treasure there like Aladdin in his cave, at our own sweet will, knowing now many things we only dimly guessed at in our much-served days—that the spires of shallots stand for orderly rows of glass jars in the store cupboard, where later globed brown bodies will jostle each other in spicy vinegar, waiting for cold-meat days to proclaim them; that the terracotta jars, like big bells, hide pale pink stalks of rhubarb, and that little round radishes, ivory and red like chessmen, will shine for us in salads and at breakfast fresher than any London folk can hope to taste.

We find new things to marvel at in our brown comrade potato, in his little leather jerkin; in the red carrots, swaggering plumed musketeers that they are; and in the sugared globe of the ruddy beet.

Asparagus, we found, is not the rare and difficult vegetable to grow which we had always fondly supposed it to be, in the light of the enormous prices pinned on the fat bundles in Piccadilly and charged for a few lorn sticks (with Hollandaise) in restaurants. Indeed, properly planted, it grows with great amiability.

Every well-made asparagus-bed has three layers of soil. About three feet down a rich stratum of farmyard manure, over that a good spit of friable (never damp or water-logged) garden soil, mixed with mortar rubbish, wood-ash and road scrapings, which must be free from motor traffic, as oil and petrol are not manures! Then, piled up over the asparagus crowns, with their budding horns so like a kid's, should come a layer of fine rich soil. Salt is an excellent treatment for this vegetable as most of us know. And I have heard it said that the asparagus which grows wild on the salt sand-dunes of Holland rivals, indeed beats, the choicest flavoured varieties grown here and in France.

I have always deeply longed to have a garden somewhere within hail of the sea. We are an Island people. I have always wanted to taste salt in my garden breezes, to know that the land I toil upon is closely lapped, torn, bruised and kissed by the furious, splendid sea. It is a source of regret to me, too, that I am not near enough to be able to put seaweed and fish-manure upon our ground; sprats, herrings, pilchards and shell fish are especially valuable to asparagus, parsnips, carrots, beets, onions and beans.

Seaweed needs to be dug in fresh, and comes under the heading of green manure. The queer kind we have all played with as children, and waded and bathed among, with little balloons all over it that it is an irresistible temptation to "pop," contains sulphate of lime and magnesia, a little phosphate of lime, and sulphate and muriate of soda. The long green ribbons we all know, the stuff that looks like oiled silk, has the valuable property of a large proportion of salts of potash as well as soda. Seaweed is a most excellent manure for potatoes.

In cutting asparagus it may be wise to point out the extreme delicacy of the operation. Clumsily cut asparagus is a garden crime of a punishable degree. A hasty, unsympathetic knife-blade hacking down into the crowns in a greedy effort to get sticks as long as possible will leave a trail of damage a good gardener's heart will bleed to see. An asparagus-cutter is, or should be, an understanding artist.

Parsnips proved much more laborious, strange to say, the first year we became intimate with the kitchen garden ; an epoch which was marked by much new knowledge in the Garden of Experience. We were accustomed to very fine parsnips on our table, as they seem to like our light warm soil. But we learned that they had vices like other things ; after they had grown to a reputable height inspection struck a chill to the heart, for we found on many leaves that dreaded brown mark (as though someone had dropped hot cigarette ash or a spot of boiling water) which on celery always means a long day's bending and picking out. A closer view disclosed the fact that every brown patch contained a maggot, just as in the celery leaves, only that those in the parsnip crop seem fatter, huskier fellows than their kin of the celery trenches ; no recommendation at all to our good will.

Where this pest is allowed to ravage unnoticed and unchecked there will presently be weeping and gnashing of teeth, for the grubs as they proceed on their destined career will finally arrive at the ground and proceed to devour the crowns of the parsnips, so that in due course where there should be a crop will be a wilderness. There is only one cure that I know of, and that is to go over the rows plant by plant, and leaf by leaf, tearing off each infected patch and burning the catch at the " end of a perfect day ! " There are compensations in this seeming deadly job as every true gardener knows. The hours beat by on a rhythmic pulse, patterned by wind and sun and rain, and in this steady toil the brain ranges free, coming back to the body refreshed and enriched. The intimate bird and bee life too will soon accept a bent back and slow-moving hands as part of the garden, and reveal their artless joys, desires and quests; till what seemed to be a small spaced task proves itself to be teeming with life and love and interest. Parsnips are a valuable crop, both from the food and harvesting point of view. They do not need clamping or storing for the winter, but can be left in the ground and lifted when and as desired, no small consideration with labour so short. Of course the nicest way to serve them is to boil them; and, when quite cooked, slice and fry them to a rich brown.

The passing of our servants has brought with it many compensations, for even if we do work harder and find leisure precious as never before, we are freed from the old tyranny of their habits and tempers, keyed to an uncomfortably different pitch from our own. We have learned to serve ourselves, and are well served, cleanly, punctually, and good-temperedly; we have learned to value, in uncommon degree, the precious gift of leisure, and to fill its moments, once so languidly easy, with the doubly distilled joy of their added value.

The habits of our little community being thus nicely edged it may well be believed that ceremonial

"Digging the holes for planting roses." Chap. XII.

"The picking of jam-fruit is the excuse for many a happy day." Chap. XIV.

JAM AND THE COOK-POTS

cleaves about the cook-pots in the fiery service of the kitchen. At any hour of any day our kitchen may be visited and an array of aluminium pans and saucepans encountered, which shine inside and out, and even beneath, like polished silver. It has become a passion, clean food, cleanly grown, cleanly cooked, cleanly served, and we are very willing to work to this end. The preserving pan, a vast shallow circle of silvery aspect with silvery handles at either side, is thick, the metal heats slowly; and retaining the heat, cooks the jam slowly and very thoroughly, while the kindly metal keeps the colour of fruit very much brighter than an iron pan will ever do.

The picking of jam fruit is the excuse for many a happy day, as hop-picking is among certain rougher folk. We have always entertained a fierce prejudice as a family for home-made jam—indeed, I think we have little patience with any machine-made or imitation conserves. A prejudice shared, I know, by most good housewives.

As the whortleberries take on their blue-black bloom in the deep gullies where they grow among the heather, baskets, dogs, babies and grown-ups collect in a splendid troop and set forth to despoil the low growing bushes away over the hill where woods and heather meet. Less adventurous souls sit in the kitchen and pick over all the beady black currants, for one of our best jams is made of $\frac{3}{4}$ lb.

sugar to ½ lb. *each* of whortleberries (commonly called " hurts " in Surrey) and black currants. The foraging party comes back at night ravenous, deeply dyed from the berries and full of tales of adventure ; one of the most melancholy I remember being that of a trustful soul who left a bobtail sheep-dog pup and two small rascals of boys to guard the day's booty. By and by mamma sheepdog appeared, and in the game that ensued the fruit was upset and lost among the heather. A lamentable story, for whortleberries, blueberries, whinberries, blackberries, or whatever fancy name you choose to call them, are slow to gather, each tiny berry from its own wee stem. Our " hurts " jam went short of whorts that year, and tasted more powerfully than it should of black currants.

One war-year, in a painful shortage of fruit, we evolved a very nice tomato jam which was quite widely used and appreciated ; here is the recipe for it. Peel 12 lb. tomatoes in the usual way, viz. by steeping in boiling water for a minute or so, then peeling. Add the juice and rind of 6 lemons, peeled very thin ; 6 oz. of hard stem ginger, bruised well with a hammer and tied into 4 little muslin bags; 8 lb. of sugar to the 12 lb. of fruit, and stand all together for 24 hours. Then boil in the usual manner of all jams, till the juice sets, and before bottling, of course, remove the bags of ginger.

Talking of ginger reminds me of our very popular

rhubarb jam, which we make in its season thus: To every pound of rhubarb ¾ lb. sugar, which are boiled together, with the rind of 9 lemons and the juice of 4 to every 12 lb. of rhubarb.

If the rhubarb is young let it simmer for three-quarters of an hour after coming to the boil; but if old, an hour to an hour and a half. Fifteen minutes before it is done, add ½ lb of Jordon almonds, blanched and chopped; and also the ginger (not the juice) from a 3-lb. jar of preserved ginger. This should be cut into small dice.

I received a lesson one day in plucking apples, which has never been forgotten.

I started out to visit the little orchard where Newton Wonder shone buxom and inviting among green leaves in a way to entice the eye of every good jam-maker; it seemed to me that the hour for picking had arrived, and in order to secure expert advice I slipped an arm in that of the girl-gardener.

We each took a basket and proceeded cheerfully to the apple trees, where the sweet-smelling fruit hung like little gorgeous lanterns in the boughs. An experienced young hand and eye travelled among them, and I learned that it was quite time for plucking. Joyfully I set forth to pull the apples and drop them into the trug, encountering immediately a pair of shocked and stormy blue eyes from between the leaves: every kind of misdeed it seemed

I had been guilty of, in my care-free handling of the fruit.

"You should treat them like eggs: put your hand under each apple gently like this, give a half-turn and it dislodges—never pull and break and never drop them in the basket. It bruises the fruit."

The shocked voice in which she uttered " bruises " gave me such a glimpse of my ignorance and ill-doing that I retired crushed to a neighbouring bank; and sat and watched the real way to collect apples, remembering much the while . . . how we used to shake the trees at home, in the old far-off days when girl-gardeners and scientific up-to-date methods were not dreamed of. The old " Persuasion " tree, for instance, full of golden pippins that mother liked and which we children were not allowed to climb or pick, the fruit was kept for her, but we were allowed the windfalls, so whenever we were near we used to " persuade " the tree a little, and most of the pippins ultimately fell our way.

I remember, too, the cider apples, big orchards in Devon and in Worcestershire where piles of bruised and fallen fruit were collected for the farmers' presses, in the roughest kind of way.

My mind ran to and fro like a shuttle between the old ways and the new: the old so careless and so wasteful, but full of a certain homely intelligence and easy generosity nevertheless; the new so economical, so brimful of science and theory, so concentrated on profit and focussed on the balance-sheet.

I watched her practised hands, swift and sure, and knew how right she was and how wrong I was, but for a traitorous second I wished myself back in the old days of the Garden of Ignorance when every act was a glowing adventure and the bogey of technical knowledge had not yet raised a whisper at me from among the leaves.

And then, far from this little pretty English orchard, my mind rolled back to others I have seen : commercial orchards scattered over the British Empire where all the arts of growing, picking, grading, packing, and marketing are practised like a religion by the orchardist settlers who make big incomes from their land. Apple orchards in Tasmania and British Columbia, vineyards and peach orchards in the beautiful Hex River Valley in South Africa—miles of perfumed orange and tangerine trees in New South Wales and sober flats of spear-like leaves in Natal, in each crown of which nestles a gold and ruddy pineapple ; a beguiling sight for thirsty travellers under the ardent sun. These tiny isles with their forty-five million inhabitants often seem very crowded to my land-hungry heart.

"There you are, darling ! It's a fine crop from two small trees," piped a voice in my ear. We staggered back to the cottage with two well-filled baskets of Newton Wonder to turn into dumplings and jam.

Our most beloved conserve is marrow jam; personally I always omit the chilies, but put them in the recipe as I received it, after a long, long hunt in many books and in many houses. The marrows must be quite ripe, almost woody, or they will boil pulpy. Cut the lemon rind exceedingly fine and leave it in the jam. First peel the marrows, remove all soft parts and seeds, and cut into squares of about one inch, and a nice job it is, too, if the marrows are really ripe; aching wrists and weariness of heart always seem to be part of cutting up marrows, unless one can get a merry soul or two to help. To every pound of marrow add 1 lb. of sugar. To every 2 lb. of marrow, add the juice and thin rind of 1 lemon. Mix and stand for 24 hours. Then add 1 oz. of hard ginger, well bruised, to every 4 lb. of marrow, and 9 pods of chilies in muslin bags. Boil an hour and a half to two hours; until, in fact, the juice is sticky—not runny and watery—and the narrow squares are transparent. Then remove the muslin bags and bottle.

This is a confection which never fails to stir the soul of all guests to greed, which is a compliment we greatly treasure.

We have developed a practice of eating our lettuce as a vegetable, and most people who have tried it say it is as much a delicacy as asparagus. The well-

JAM AND THE COOK-POTS

cleaned lettuces are dropped into boiling water which has been well salted and has a good pinch of bicarbonate of soda in it. They boil till tender (about twenty minutes), and then require very careful straining. Our way is to lift them whole half an hour before the rest of the meal is ready, and put them in their vegetable dish in a warm corner of the stove rack. Every ten minutes or so the water which has accumulated should be emptied off. When everything else is ready a dash of butter, to gloss the top, and a grind of pepper, and lo! a most delicious and uncommon dish.

We had a goose given us one day—a live one. It had a sentimental way of looking at us and followed us about like a dog; but it had been used to living in a troop, or herd, or whatever they call goose families, and when left alone it cried out in the most heartbroken way, annoying a neighbour lady (with an imagination) who lives in the valley. So we had to kill the poor goose, which made us sad, for we rather loved its silly face. When I went forth to get sage to stuff him with, I was forcibly reminded of the tiresome way some people have of picking sage. It ought never to be cropped all over the top so as to leave the branches naked or stumpy. Servants are mostly too lazy to care how they pull herbs. When sage is two years old or more a dressing of very old dry manure may be lightly forked in with profit.

It is the herb that, I suppose, is most limited in its vocation. Somehow it never seems to belong anywhere but inside a duck, or a goose. Yet it should be used liberally in garden decoration, for it does make a most wonderful effect in a colour scheme, especially when the handsome purple bloom is out among the silvery grey leaves. We grow the sage borders from seed, sowing it in April, in rich, light earth, in drills a quarter of an inch deep and six inches apart. The seedlings get thinned out in due course, and in the following autumn are removed to their final growing place.

We use our gooseberries in rather unorthodox ways, despising them as jam, and greatly admiring them in wine, or as pickle. The pickle takes very little sugar and makes a fine addition to cold meat days and " chutney " for curries. We make it thus : Six lb. of gooseberries, 2½ lb. of sugar, ½ oz. of ground cloves, 1 pint (not more) of vinegar should be placed into an enamelled pan and boiled (stirred the while) into the thickness of jam. Bottle as jam.

Gooseberry wine matures after being two or three years in bottle into a very wholesome and pleasant wine, rather of the Moselle type. Boil 3 lb. of lump sugar in a gallon of water for about twenty minutes. When nearly cold add 4 quarts of ripe bruised gooseberries, and stand altogether for a couple of days, stirring at intervals. Then dissolve ½ oz. of isinglass in a pint of brandy, and add the whites of five eggs, whisking both well together for half an hour.

Strain the wine through flannel into a cask, add the isinglass and egg whisk, and stir all together. After corking the cask place it in a cool place for six months, then bottle off for use. A lump of sugar and two raisins must be placed in each bottle.

Among our cook-pots we learned that there are certain kitchen economies which, faithfully rendered to our garden, come back to us a hundredfold in finer fruits and vegetables. The sweep, crafty merchant, removes the soot if one is too lazy or too unlearned to order him to leave his valuable plunder, take his legitimate fee and begone.

The actual ingredients of soot are as follows, if my memory serves me well: Charcoal, 371; Salts of Ammonia, 426; Salts of Potash and Soda, 24; Oxide of Iron, 50; Silica, 65; Alumina, 31; Sulphate of Lime, 31; Carbonate of Magnesia, 2. It is wise to remember that soot is too stimulating a diet for plants when they are quiescent and that the proportion in which to use it for garden crops is six quarts of soot to a hogshead of rain water. In that form it is a cause of great rejoicement to asparagus, peas, onions, carrots and all the rest of the useful brigade. It acts on them like champagne on humans—makes them light up and become active and brilliant.

Potash manures are necessary, as we all know, to

good cultivation, but not every amateur gardener knows that turf, hedge-trimmings, prunings, etc., when burned will supply potash in the ashes ; they should be spread over the soil at once before the virtue has departed. Goats make short work of many a large armful of prunings and trimmings which would otherwise burn itself into potash manure. A Horsfall destructor is most useful in producing ash with manurial value from the household and garden rubbish. I believe most thoroughly in burning the dustbin contents instead of burying. For one thing it saves labour. I often used to grieve to watch the gardener emptying and burying the house refuse, and before I heard of the destructor I had to resolutely close my eyes to the obvious breeding ground that the refuse dumps made for our common enemy the fly. The heat generated by the burning rubbish can be used to heat water ; and there is an economical joy, that is almost a radiance, in destroying something bad and creating something useful in one and the same act.

CHAPTER XIV

LOVERS IN THE GARDEN

> . . . War knows no power, safe shall be my going,
> Secretly armed against all death's endeavour;
> Safe though all safety's lost; safe where men fall;
> And if these poor limbs die, safest of all.
>
> RUPERT BROOKE.

ONE of the prides of our garden is the summer show of hollyhocks down both sides of a grass path; tall stems of them grow sloping towards the south, lit up in their season from base to tip with multi-coloured silken blooms. I love the single hollyhocks, and grow them from seed, which is the reason, I am told, that they flourish so well here, and do not succumb to that disease which almost killed the cult of hollyhocks some years ago, when they were a vigorous fancy. I do not remember it, but hear tales of the passionate pursuit of new varieties and the tremendous rage for hollyhocks, mostly the double ones, which prevailed long ago in the fashionable world of gardeners; a vogue as violent as the tulip boom, or the passion for pansies. Inbreeding and grafting were the downfall of double hollyhocks into the slough of disease ; proof again that nature must be comrade, and never enslaved . . . she is murderously resentful of coercion. The greatest lover in the world she is, giving all of herself to those who woo her ; but to the taskmaster, or the forgetful, revenge incarnate.

Fortunately for myself, I prefer the wide silken saucers of the natural single hollyhocks, caring little for the tight, hard rosettes of the double ones ; so I stumbled into my mother Nature's pleasure at once, and she gives me royally year after year banners of purple and cream, yellow and rose, flame and crimson.

They always remind me of a romance. Once, among my week-end guests I spied with all the sympathy of world-wayfarer, a leaning on the part of a brilliant young scientist for the company of a blue-eyed lady. So one morning I sent them for a long walk through the woods to get me some meadow-sweet for house decoration. I told them the way very carefully, being pretty sure I should never see the meadow-sweet, which is not stuff I care for indoors anyway, as it has a heavy scent . . . and they were lost for hours. Towards dinner-time I found a conscience-stricken couple hastily arranging hollyhocks in a big pitcher, and learned that they had never got further than the seat under the beech tree at the bottom of the kitchen garden, having forgotten the time ! They came in for some teasing from the rest of the party in spite of my efforts to protect them, because the hollyhocks gave them away. Time went on, and my cherished friend, the scientist, began to look pale and wan; the lady was reluctant and indecisive; his affection was heavily involved, and I suggested he tried his fortune and put the matter to the test. The result was unfortunate. When war broke out he went without so much as a farewell to anyone, to fight with the desperation of a man who is looking for a bullet. His career as a soldier was exceptionally brilliant; and one day I received a letter which touched me very much, asking me to accept a bar to the Military Cross and the Insignia of the Distinguished Service Order in the name of my garden, where he had learned the meaning of happiness, and which had stood to him in many a lone vigil for the England he fought for. I met the lady he loved soon afterwards; and was telling her of this letter, when our host looked up from his newspaper to say, " Poor Ernest is killed." In the stricken face which turned to me I saw that too late she had learned where her heart had been, and in my sorrow at the passing of a very fine spirit I felt cold resentment at her vanity and coquetry.

Many moons after I invited a select party of two down to the Cottage-of-Dreams-come-True. One was a repentant siren, the other a much decorated soldier with five wound stripes on his sleeve, who had been very decently treated by the Hun doctors after being left for dead in one of the terrible battles of spring, 1918, when England " stood with her back to the wall " and the fate of civilisation trembled in the balance. In the parlour, it being August once again, I placed a large pitcher of hollyhocks. And there they met alone. . . .

There have been many lovers in my garden. I love them all and rejoice when they come again in the tide of years with their babies to renew the glamour of the courting days.

There are some things I am not allowed to have in the garden. One of them is a " popular." I have admired them for many years. The tall slim poplars, slender yet significant, remind me of the harp in orchestra. For some reason I always hear music in a landscape ; and see vast landscapes when I am at the Opera ; as though it were Nature thinking aloud. The strong and slender poplars please me much ; they accent the composition of a scene as the exclamation point does a dashing phrase in literature. And I have another reason, purely personal, for loving them. In the bitter years I drove a gallant man back to camp one misty dawn through miles of rolling South country, phrased with pine and pointed here and there with poplar trees. The cold, low-lying mist clung about our faces. The wounded man beside me was going straight back to the Front, and at that hour every farewell uttered by the women of Britain had in its core the bitterness of Death. My fingers so ached with the cold that they would hardly turn the steering wheel; the sculptor-soldier's silent face looked blue and pinched. Just as we stopped near the camp, and had exchanged our last handclasp and steady glance the sun wore through the mist and a long, slim shadow lit up the road. I turned once more, and saw—as I shall see for ever—the tents rising out of the mist, and a sentinel poplar swaying gently to the dawn wind; in its pale shadow the motionless figure of the soldier at salute.

So I love poplars. But I may not have one in the garden. The gardener has other ideas. "Nasty things, they populars; they be greedy, eating up everything, and where will you find the water for 'em on this hillside?"

Yet, if I had one here at my door the strong sad memory of that sacramental hour would never become a matter of course; nor the sound of its "morituri" beat less poignant in the heart.

The cenotaph in Whitehall is tall and slender; in the dawn it must cast a long, pale shadow too. . . .

I do not know who first thought of the shrines that are now scattered through the length and breadth of our Isles, in memory of the deathless who have passed from the sight of man these last five years, but it was a sympathetic human whoever he was; for, small though the remnant of such comfort is, it is a comfort to the grieving to give tangible blossoms and living tears to a tablet of memory. For years that usual piteous comfort was far from our reach. Spattered across the battlefields of Europe, unmarked, untended, desperately out of reach were the graves we desired to honour. The unpretentious shrines that have been erected by so many parish communities were conceived in alleviation of that pain.

Some of the shrines are commonplace and ugly. I suspect them of being factory made, uninspired in design and craftmanship. Ours in this village is very simple and very dignified; in its grief it has the merit of thoughtfulness and therefore of beauty. There are some elect souls in this, the prettiest town in Surrey, who have taste and imagination and the courage to express them; so our shrine was designed locally by Harold Falkner, architect and disabled soldier, and carried out in locally grown woods. Essentially a home-tribute to men who had gone out to fight for home. Upon one panel is a war speech by Sir Nigel Loring, a local warrior of Plantagenet days, and on the other, part of Rupert Brooke's sonnet "Safety," to link the whole emblem with the wider brotherhood of man. In the space between the panels are lists of all the serving men of our village, with a mark beside each whose owner has been sacrificed. Below, a leaden vessel contains water for the flowers which are always kept fresh by the villagers, many of whom satisfy a dumb, deep sense of poetry by choosing flowers of special significance—heart's-ease, forget-me-not, pansies, ivy, and rosemary.

Living near the little shrine as I do, watching it and the constant silent tenderness that flows about it, I am sure that it is good. It is a peg to hang dreams upon; every stricken soul who lingers there has a chance to win back vision, to glimpse again the great perspective; to feel that what it gave it has; that the name inscribed there is beyond tarnish; honourable in the history of men and imperishable in love.

The desire to do homage to soldier dead is very old; I was startled to learn recently how old. During the summer holiday I was taken into a tiny church in Monmouthshire close to the Usk. On the wall was a stone which had been found near by, and embedded in the wall of the church. It was to one "Julianus," a soldier of the 2nd Legion, A.D. 75, who was "40 years of age and had served for 17 years, placed to his memory by a beloved wife." Beside it was a very white new marble tablet placed by grieving parents to the memory of their two soldier sons lost but now in France. Eighteen hundred and forty-four years between the two; the same profession of arms and the same grief.

In London City, between Charing Cross and Westminster, midway in the tide of feet between Nelson's pillar and the mother of Parliaments, in the heart-core of our nation's history, is now set the shrine of shrines ; the spot dedicate ; a few feet of a London thoroughfare which is holy ground.

The cenotaph is our nation's gesture of reverence to the dead ; the " frozen sigh " of all mourning women ; free from creed-mark and majestic as birth or as death in its naked simplicity. Victorious armies of half the world have done it honour ; bitter splendid France, little Italy, stubborn Belgium, Poland, Portugal, Serbia, Roumania, classic Greece, apostolic America, inscrutable China, Japan, and far Siam ; all these and our own matchless Empire, gathered from vast dominions all over the globe, rendered it tribute on the day of the celebration of Peace. Ever since, a constant pilgrimage has been made, as to a holy island in the sea of traffic. Aching hearts go homing there. The unquenchable spirit of man flames from that high altar, set among a city's hurrying feet.

CHAPTER XV

DROUGHT IN THE GARDEN

*Love that so desires would fain keep her changeless
Fain would fling the net, and fain have her free.*
                              GEORGE MEREDITH

ONE year autumn delayed her coming, and summer was fierce in the land. Field and garden, man and beast, were baked to a suffering drought; the hot airs came to our lungs unrefreshingly, as though they were met by the breath of an open furnace.

The usually resonant pines, sensitive as wind-harps to the least sigh of a breeze, were still; heavily mute; stretching tensely up to a merciless sky. We listened longingly for a sound of their persistent usual murmuring, knowing that the first purr among their topmost boughs is advent of a breeze. Their unaccustomed silence chilled the heart with a sense of loss, like the passing of a loved loquacious neighbour; the unfamiliar stare they turned to the stars, stark and rigid, was as revolting to us as frozen death itself; to us who knew divinely well the living flowing grace of their daily companionship.

The lawns were slippery and brown; the silken hollyhocks were scorched; roses, lavender, lettuces, peas, beans and a host of other trusty friends gasped sadly on the hot and hungry sand. My gardener-mother-heart grieved, and I hated my helplessness. It was hard to see the flower-children pass before their time, when both the hands of hope were held out to welcome them and love them through their bud and bloom. Their little lives are short at best, and in years of drought they are most cruelly shortened. Friends fled gasping from blistered London-town, to sleep in hammocks and camp beds under the pines. Scorched though it was, I could rejoice in the garden still, for it harboured a thankful crowd those days.

Away in one corner two industrious creatures were spending perspiring but happy hours attending to the goats. They had bathed the kids, and were now slaving with saw and plane upon long planks of oak, making a very elegant milking stool, which is a joy in the goathouse still, though the hot spell has long passed, and the carpenters returned to the sophistications of town. No one would have guessed, to look at them, that they were two well-known literary men.

Anyone who has tried to milk a little goat from the ground will realise what a convenience some sort of platform is for the operation. The animals run to their stool and jump up eagerly night and morning,

"Making the goats' milking-stool." *Chap. XVI*

DROUGHT IN THE GARDEN

putting their heads through the bars, which then close lightly, as they know that a bowl of bran and oats is set in the opening under their noses. And there they munch delectably while the milker sits alongside and milks at ease.

In a shady corner beneath the "crocus hill" an ardent group was trying to bleach some Government linen, dashing out at frequent intervals from the vantage coign of shade to spray and turn the fabric spread out in the blazing sun. Violent controversy raged as to the progress of the bleaching, and fragments of linen wisdom were wafted through the study window to me from time to time:

"I like this quality best; it is so fine that I shall make frocks of it and blouses too."

"I have the heavy 'T' quality, and I am making sheets of it. I shall keep them brown and embroider my monogram on them; then I shall put a black satin quilt over the bed" drifted in upon me next in a rich housewife voice; and presently piped another which I know well: "I shall make breeches and smocks out of mine for gardening in, and hand them down to my great-grandchildren as relics of exquisite Georgian handiwork . . ."

I heard no more of the linen talk. I turned to brood wonderingly on a vision of my child with great-grandchildren!

Away in the deeps of bracken were the "demobbed" soldier-friends, frankly sleeping out the heat of the day on scented pine needles ; even the welcome cry of tea, which had enticed linen-mongers and carpenters indoors, did not break the deep repose of their young limbs.

I put away my writing presently, and crept out of doors the back way to avoid being seen. I wanted to be alone, to sit in the sun and think, without the voices of friends to break into a brooding hour. I slipped down the lane, shady, sequestered, past the field where the goats lay cudding contentedly, down to the gate in the wood ; I climbed a brackened slope and scrambled up a big tree to a comfortable familiar bough, whence I could survey the valley from thickets of sheltering green. Away near the croquet lawn faint sounds of saw and hammer murmured soothingly of the carpenters' insatiable industry, and now and again a distant laugh floated up from scattered groups like a smothered chime. It was a peaceful afternoon, and I gratefully settled down to useless but absorbing thoughts of the valley life below ; how the centuries roll by folding generation after generation into the earth, while still the spade and the sword alternately heal and scar her face ; how the lens of life focuses for the peasants on the ancient church beside the hill where they take their young brides for marriage, later their children for baptism, and last of all are borne themselves for burial to wait, with patient feet turned toward the dawn, to learn what

DROUGHT IN THE GARDEN

each must learn of death, after life has been proven.

Across the privet hedge where the quince stood like a sentinel, way down among fruit trees, a globular form bobbed and swayed about some business. I guessed it was a cottager hiving a very late swarm of bees, because I had seen her broad hat garnished with a black veil going toward the orchard as I climbed my tree. And if I had doubted her mission with only that evidence a tall spire of smoke from the bee-bellows in one hand and the familiar outline of a swarm-box in the other had told their tale. I watched her lazily: it was very good to be alone. I rejoiced in the peaceful companionship of birds and flowers, and the filtered glances of the sun. A click at the gate into the wood snapped across my thoughts like the crack of a whip. A khaki-clad figure was entering, tall, broad-shouldered, loose-limbed. With all my earnest joy at seeing him again, safe and whole from France, my spirit quailed at the invasion. For the strenuous personality of that Californian always wrought mightily among my peaceful moods.

I peered down on his progress, weakly hoping for a reprieve from the ardours of his welcoming grip. But the hand of God was upon me, and I was at that moment delivered of a lusty sneeze. He turned his pleasant sunburned face up, alight with his magnetic smile. How attractive young

Americans are. "Gee, it's good to be back!" he said.

"And it's good to see you," I answered, truthfully enough. "Will you come up here and rest awhile?"

But not so our Westerner; he did not want to sit and dream, he was all for walking about. His former visits to the cottage had been rich in illumination; and we had received from his unconscious hands a liberal education in the attributes of his race. My indolent introspection was stung to attention; he was active as a squirrel, and I must needs walk the garden with him. Most of us Britons had heard, or read, of the ravenous intelligence of these newest armies in our midst; and here I had it naked and unashamed. I clambered down to joust with him in tourney of question and answer with what valour I might summon at a moment's notice; and a breathless job it was. We found ourselves presently by the quince tree, and his sharp eye spied the activities of my peasant neighbour.

"Has Mrs. Jones gone to collect a swarm of bees?" he asked.

"Yes," I answered, caught at once in the toils of controversy.

"Sure it's late for that, and anyway it's a cast, not a swarm!" he exclaimed; and when I agreed, but reminded him how we are fighting the Isle of

Wight Disease, which has almost blotted out our native stocks in the last few years, by importing Dutch and Italian bees which are much given to swarming, he looked at me unimpressed. I repeated my " credo." " Swarming bees are better than dead bees."

" Mr. Harry W. Beaver out where I come from imports a hundred pure Italian queen-bees every year, and he knows how to head off swarming fever. He tries to avoid swarming altogether, and increases by the nucleus instead. This old lady don't have a system, I guess."

I suggested that his friend might be a bee-farmer and expert ; that bees were only a side-line here. But that was no use. . . .

" He's an expert sure enough, but he ain't my friend. I've only heard of him. He's of the Middle-West. But what about Mrs. Ardele Packard ? Her bees are only a side-line, but she would be worried sick if she had casts out now."

As I didn't know the lady I had to subside.

" She made nine hundred dollars from her bees last year, but she has a system," pursued the relentless critic.

I accused him of being an expert in disguise, but he turned upon me his dazzling smile . . . we loved our Californian's smile, it had the irradiance of perfect health and spirits.

" Never touched a hive till I made yours ! " He

declared, and then paused before the border of catmint and snapdragon.

"What's that?" he asked. "It's mighty pretty."

I reflected hurriedly. I knew the terrible efficiency of our American doughboy—he was always keeping my National pride out of breath . . . this highly educated lad would probably only know the horticultural names of our flowers which (for all I knew) might be world-wide, while our pretty country names would probably be only local to these Isles. As usual I made an effort to hold our end up, and replied:

"Nepeta Mussini and Antirrhinum Nelrose."

He considered a moment and passed on. . . .

"What's that?—it looks like sea-anemone!"

I approved his happy simile; the scarlet fringe of bergamot is very like the sea-anemones one may find in the clear green depths of a still sea-pool. We gossiped of its use in distilling perfumes, and he pinched a leaf to sniff at, much edified. A tall, broad-leaved stem, carrying a wilted treasure, next filled his eye. He looked at me.

"Iris Pallida Dalmatica," I announced glibly; again he passed on.

"I know this," he said, brushing his hand lovingly through the bushes of fragrant purple lavender; "but what do you call that?" pointing over the hedge, where the thriftless bee-woman still pursued her shameful work ; with an artist's soul somewhere submerged in her ample frame she had planted a large collection of blue herbaceous stuff against the background of honey-scented purple Buddleia ; a clump of Delphiniums, some anchusas, a large group of fluttering bells, and it was on these his eye was fixed.

"It's Campanula Persicœfolia, Telham Beauty."

"*We* call them Canterbury Bells," he declared, and I welcomed his news with great relief. "So do we," I said, "and these were flags, and these snapdragons, and this is sea-holly. . . ."

"And those are roses," he chuckled. "We have easier names for our flowers than you, where I come from ! Gee, it's good to be back ! "

I stepped hurriedly off the high pedestal of grand names and joined him in whole-hearted comradeship on the common ground of flower names ; though the late swarm that was taking so much of Mrs. Jones' time still rankled in my mind. It was a disgrace to good bee-keeping, as much a disgrace as a septic finger to a trained nurse, and I felt my country was let down by her sloppy methods. This boy, I reflected, must live in a highly efficient land, actively opposed to dreamers and wasters. It annoyed me to have to smart silently under his perfectly justifiable remarks ; I felt I wanted to brace up and show off in some way to get things level. However, I took a long draught of that heady and dangerous drink, national complacency, as we trod the trim paths of the kitchen garden, edged neatly with pot-herbs. Here my American frankly praised.

"I always love your truck-garden. Americans get their vegetables out of tins mostly," he admitted, gazing at the rows of drought-stricken vegetables. "I guess it's because they have their land to break and clear in the Middle-West. They don't do much gardening. They have their crops to sow, and the women have too much housework to do to want to bother with vegetable gardens."

"We eat fresh vegetables in this country," I swanked. "We do not wage the tremendous war on microbes that you do as a nation, but we armour ourselves from within by the vitamines contained in fresh green food, and we are a healthy race."

"You find your gardens made, your land cleared, you only have to keep it up," he reasoned. "In Pennsylvania you can see something like these old English houses because they have had a long start in settling; there are old farmhouses there, very old, and gardens; but they had three hundred years' start. They are clearing and sowing still in the Middle-West, and labour is scarce." His eye roamed round wistfully: "I hope some day they will have gardens, too. This is pretty, sure!"

Mrs. Jones came along the path, very flustered at having lost a small "cast"; and anxious to bob a curtsey to the soldier-man. Her felicitations were incommoded by the smells of Dandy, who had to be frequently shooed away. Whenever he finds a special piece of dirt to roll in he thinks he is Beau Brummell and gets above himself; wants to share his perfume and fawn on everyone. The clatter of our converse eventually roused the whole company, which hurried from every corner of the garden to welcome the soldier. His laughing glance sparkled from face to face till it found the frank beam of a girl-gardener's blue eye. And rested there.

I slipped indoors to prepare extra baked meats for dinner, an affair of bricks without straw as every war-worn housewife knew; and on my way met the Art Critic, returned from a hot and tiring day in town. We compared notes, as I tore crisp lettuce leaves apart, and beat up our famous mayonnaise without eggs; he had been talking to a Belgian " Agronome," and was delighted with the new word. His literary humour played with it like a juggler with plates, or a child with a new ball, and I laughed to hear him.

" What have you been doing all day ? " he asked at last.

" I set out to be Mary; but the Californian has come back on leave and so I am Martha," I said.

I felt a hand, thin as tears, rest for a second on my bent head and then my friend made a totally irrelevant remark. " San Francisco is quite close really; only twelve days away."

When the " heather-moon," the " honey " moon, the August moon rolled a great red-gold rim out of the East pushing long shadows of the pine trunks in front of her through the wood, the whole party betook itself, refreshed and tremendous with energy, to the lawn. A gramophone was brought out, and presently " Destiny " made an irresistible call to dancing feet. Lewis and I sat back and watched them in deep content; in and out of the shadowed spaces the couples swung over the dry and slippery grass. The morris dancer, slim as a wand, dark-browed and tall, spun by, hopelessly tangled in the sailorman's willing efforts to emulate the gunner, who, with the help of the Only-Woman-in-the-World, was squirming industriously in the astounding convolutions of the " Jazz." Lurking round the laurels we could espy the General intent on waylaying his coy Daphne who had fled him for too long. The two carpenters were doing shadow-dances together near the sundial; snatches of Western lore came our way as Lewis's wife whirled by in the untiring arms of her fellow-countryman, our American " lonely " soldier.

The Art Critic's pointed beard jutted out against the moonlight; his eyes glittered, darkly brown, in the rays, and his presence filled the night with deep content. He is the kind of man whose friendship fills life like the air one breathes, as unobtrusive and as vital to soul-health.

"God knows they've earned their play," he said at last, as if half to himself. "There is not a creature here but has 'played the game' these bitter years of war, and most of the men bear the mark on their bodies. Dicky left the artillery for the Air Force and crashed in a riddled plane in France, he lay paralysed for two years; West spent ten months in bed recovering from a bayonet wound in the body; the General has a shattered hand; and our Secret Service pal by the sundial has a bullet in his leg . . . neither shirker nor profiteer has a place in your garden, my dear."

I listened, and did not listen. The dancers were changing partners, in spite of the gunner's efforts to secure a third encore, and I could see the American firmly changing records. Determined lad. I wondered what his mother might be like. Somewhere in this world of ours, a sister-woman had done her man-making well, with pride and with love she had wrought; somewhere in this world, a Western mother's heart was longing for him at this moment, as his did, I well knew, for her. My love, unknown, flowed out on a deep and piteous tide of understanding. I could feel the intense ray of her eyes, so tender and so exacting, beating across the void to her boy wherever he might go. I wished I knew her.

The gramophone began "Missouri," and on the wings of that throbbed sweetness the American took a golden-headed girl on his arm with the air of a king.

. . . . .

When the moon had climbed high above the pine-tops and the whole land lay glamoured beneath her, cigarettes began to spark like glow-worms from point to point, where dance-wearied feet turned to the hammocks, and my household slept under the stars through the livelong splendid night.

CHAPTER XVI

HALLOW E'EN

> And where go you. . . . O worn and weary dear
> Who loved the stars, and laughed beneath the leaves?
> Unbroken heart that could not lean on fear,
> But saw the stars, and laughed beneath the leaves.

DANDY is convinced I am going to the cinema; it is seven o'clock and he sees me locking up the house. The cinema habit appears to be growing upon me nowadays, and we often go down together to the town for an evening's entertainment—he and I. I explain to him that we have an assignation this evening at "The Bush" to dine with the Art Critic and his wife, a farewell banquet of three, as they sail for America to-morrow; but he does not believe a word of it, and stops to gossip with the Albino Pekinese at the top of the hill by the pillar-box. Presently we encounter an incongruous couple, a timorous old spinster chaperoned from possible perils of foot-pads and admirers by the company of a young and lively wire-haired terrier. I eye their approach with mistrust. The fellow pulls his burden after him on a lead, looking for all the world like a Belgian draught dog tugging a milk cart up a hill, his square punishing jaw is well ahead of him, sniffing for mischief; he is a bundle of hard muscle, sharp teeth, and belligerent will most unhappily linked with the mild female at his rear. She leans back and he leans forward, both panting in their diverse ways. Dandy stiffens, spying his meat. Being a hooligan he has no chivalry for an enemy incommoded by a lead. Hurriedly I snatch him up, while he struggles and sobs in a fearful temper.

"Go on!" I urge her. But the maiden is so terrified by Dandy's gnashing jaws and horrible yells that she lets go of the lead and her protector hurls himself upon me, fondly believing this is bait I hold aloft. For a dizzy moment I nourish a dogfight in my arms, and then a tangled mass of white bristles and tan silk falls to the ground and rolls in front of a passing motor. It draws up with a squeal of brakes, and the chauffeur springs to my help—we disentangle the warriors, place a chewed and slimy lead in the hand of the lady in the hedge—and Dandy struts on snarling furiously till a wolfhound bitch towers on the horizon and he plunges after her to announce a gallant hope. What with his fights and flirtations I am ten minutes late; and am greeted in consequence with a very harsh frown from my old friend Frank, the waiter. "It

"Better here, in the wan moonlight—the valley below swimming full of mist." *Chap. XVII.*

was a very good sole and Mrs. Fisher chose it for you herself," he complains, ushering me into the beautiful old dining-room with its cream walls and daffodil curtains, and the sundial on an oak-beamed ceiling.

Under the light of shaded candles, shining on Michaelmas daisies, we talk of old days as friends are wont to do who are about to part. Everybody we know seems to be leaving this overtaxed Island, adventuring out to kinder and more spacious lands; Dickie is in Calcutta, George West in Burma planting teak, the morris dancer and the sailor are farming in New Zealand, the General and his hard-won beauty are spreading wings for South Africa; on every hand, among all one's friends, one hears tales of these flittings far afield. Lewis asks after the playwright and the cats, so I show them his last letter from Brazil, where he grows them to the complete astonishment of the natives on a thousand acre farm in Bahia. As the cobwebbed Port becomes imminent I am conscious that I am about to be forgiven for being late, and that Frank will soon cease to scowl at me; Mr. Fisher has dug up one of his very special bottles for the occasion, and the nice old waiter becomes quite human and friendly as he hands it round, murmuring tales of its quality from glass to glass; by the time the rich wine reaches our lips he is full of anxious sympathetic interest and all is well. Presently they tell us the car is ready to go to the station; I see them into it, sending countless messages to my girl. Hetty's blue eyes, warm with understanding, touch my eyes, and turn away; Lewis's slender hand takes mine—and they are gone. I turn into the empty misty streets preceded by Dandy, engorged and very positive, who straightway makes for the cinema. I do not argue with him, one gets a sense of companionship, of kinship with our common world in a Picture Palace. The little fellow settles himself contentedly among the smells of many feet, disregarding the screen while he waits for the sound he always recognises, when "God Save the King" frees him for the pleasures of the walk home, beset with its absorbing social endeavours.

To-night I choose the longest road back, by Moor Park and Waverley Abbey, past the Witch's Cave and the Mill Race near Stella's Cottage. The mists in the river meadow gleam like pale amethyst. Dandy sniffs and snorts along mile after mile, till at last we climb from the valley of the Spotted Cow to my garden gate. It is midnight. This is All Hallow's Eve—the wood looms up pine-pillared like a great crypt; pale spires of mist eddy softly through, and long fingers of moonlight clasp them thinly as they pass. Dandy shuffles through the gold-brown bracken, making for the front door with its promise of welcoming warmth; I do not hurry. There is no need. Better here in the little wood on the hill in the wan moonlight with the valley below swimming full of mist. There is company here, for this is the night of the dead. Millions of soundless feet move through the world to-night, millions of laughing feet that once marched away in clouds of golden dust. Glimmering faintly away in the flagged garden is the lead boy, young Pan, so young, on his rose-wreathed ball. It is the night of the dead ; beloved men and women gather here, surely, to touch my warm human heart that cries to them. Mabel, gracious, beautiful and sweet-hearted friend ; whimsical Dolly asleep under Devon heather ; the patient, loyal, simple heart of my father . . . they are here to-night, I feel, see, hear them all around. And Another, the lantern of whose body was lit with so bright a spirit . . . greater than the loving which I dare not remember was the losing for which I thank him yet.

Dandy's impatient bark crackles through the cold mist ; I go indoors, preceded by his industrious tail, and Tatty-Bogle rises, yawning, from a spent fire. He squints at me affectionately ; I take him upstairs in my arms to bed. Through the long night I hear a rose tapping its morse message on the window-sill, where a thorny spray has grown through the open window. I know my lesson now. Experience has taught me at last. I who have loved my garden am myself a garden, Time was the gardener and out of my clay grew a flower; I have borne my flower and presently I must drop back to earth and become still. This is the Awe-time of life; the profound and fruitful slumber of winter awaits me where new lessons surely will be learned.

For the Awe-time is the Hope-time in a garden.

INDEX

ALL HALLOWS EVE, the night of the dead, 308, 309
America, garden not wanted in, 105; mixed races of, 117
American architecture, poetry in, 109
Americans, kindness to, 51; incredible toilers, 107
Anchusas, 26, 297
Animals, educational use of, 43
Antirrhinum Nelrose, 296
Apple tree: "Persuasion," 272
Apples, lesson in gathering, 272
Arabis, 71, 146
Armistice, the, 23
Art Critic, 87, 93, 299, 300; I dine with, 303
Ascension Isle, rock gardens of, 110
Asparagus, origin of, 34; how to bed, 263; how to cut, 264
Asters, 245, 307
Aubretia, variety of: Doctor Mules, 27
"Auld Lang Syne," singing of, 219
Australia, picnic in, 116–119
Awe-time, 68–78; description of, 68, 69
Azaleas, 27, 113; in Natal, 114

BATTERY HILL, Rye, story of, 238
Beans, 288
Beatty, Admiral, 108

Beauty lovers, 11
Beaver, Mr. Harry W., 295
Belgium, 280
Bee-keeper, assistance of, 139, 145
Bees, 136–66; arrival of first colony, 138; in broom-time, 141; ceremonials of, 142; our first swarm, 143; supplies for, 145, 146; disliked by gardeners, 147; "domesticated animals," 156
Belloc, Hilaire, 17
Bergamot, 296
Bide, Mr., nursery of, 234; visit to, 239
Bird-yard, the, 157; birds in, 158
Black currants, 270
Blood-test, importance of, 67
Blossom buds, encouragement of, 29
Borders: Tulips, 73; roses, 121; irises, 190; catmint, 296; snapdragon, 296
Box-hedge, 11
British Bee-keeper's Guide, The, instruction from, 143
British Goat Society, 172
Brooke, Rupert, 89, 90, 279, 284; Canadian reads from, 94
Browning, 90
Buddleia, 297

Bulbs, 71, 72; choice of, 73-77; English and Spanish, 73

CABBAGE ROSE, origin of, 34
Californian, the, 51; delight of, 52; his interest in bees, 52; steeped in bee-lore, 52; "Candy" shortage of, 54; his questioning, 55; his intention to make hives, 55; his energy, 56; makes goat-stalls, 176; back on leave, 293; my thoughts of his mother, 307
Call of the blood, 11
Campanula, 26
Canterbury Bells, 146, 297
Carmen, Bliss, 136, 188
Carpenter, Edward, 79, 209
Catalogues, 73; Mr. Bide's, 76
"Cathedral of the Forest," story of, 121
Catmint, 26
Cenotaph, nations render tribute to, 286
Chaffinch, 22; mating of, 158
Cheiranthus: Pamela Purshouse, 244
Chelsea Flower Show, yearly pilgrimage to, 24
Childhood, boredom of, 36-38
Cinerarias, 27
Clematis, 245
Cootamundra, 118
Countryman's Diary, extract from, 141, 142
Courtesy, effect of, 56
Clover honey, 52
Cowan, 52
Cranesbill, 246

Crocuses, 73, 146; varieties of: Bleu Celeste, 75; King of the Whites, 75; Purpureus Grandiflorus, 75
Cytisus Præcox, 192

DAFFODIL, varieties of: King Alfred, 74; Sir Watkin, 74
Dandy: arrival of, 80; conduct of, 83, 87; missing, 101; condition when found, 102; quarrel with Tatty-Bogle, 251; unfair contest, 304; at the cinema, 308; disturbs a reverie, 309
Delphinium, 26, 297
Digging, varieties of, 33, 34
"Dipper," treatment of, 47
"Divining Rod, The," 165
Domestic duties, difficulty with, 210-14
Dormouse, as pet, failure of experiment, 45
Dream garden, 123
Drought, results from, 287, 288
Dunsany, Lord, 106
Dutch farmhouses, *see* South Africa, 112-113

EARTH-LIFE, drink at well of, 10
Edwards, Tickner, 52

FALKNER, Harold, architect, 284
Fibres, 28
Filbert, description of, 32, 33
Fitzgerald, 90
Flags, 297
Flower-beds, arrangement of, 26
Flying-fish, 110
Food supplies, scarcity of, 167
Fortune-telling, 215; list of "fates," 220-26

INDEX

GARDEN, true selves discovered in a, 49; city friends in a, 243
Garden of Ignorance, The, 7, 57, 123, 131, 197
Garden of Ignorance, days of the, 273
Gardens in: Nantucket Island, 109; Philadelphia, 109; Swampscote, 109; St. Helena, 110; Wales, 124; Sussex, 124
Gentlewoman, The, Editor of, 9
Girl-friend, visit to, 161, 162
Goat, tuberculosis unknown to, 172
Goat-farm, visit to, 184–86
Goat World, The, 169
Gooseberry: pickle, recipe for, 276; wine, recipe for, 276, 277
Great Unhappy, the, 71
Griffin, Captain, 123
Guelder rose, avenue of, 71

HAWTHORN, avenue of, 71
Heather honey, 52, 145
Henley, W. E., 49
Herbs, 198; herb-mixture, recipe for, 198; special uses for, 199–203; sow in April, 203
Hollyhocks, 279, 288; romance concerning, 280–82
Hook, Mr. Bryan, 178
Hooligan, the: *see* Dandy, 83
Horsfall destructor, usefulness of, 278
Housewives' conscience, 168
Hyacinth, varieties of: Baroness Van Tuyl, 76; Count Andrassy, 76; La Victoire, 76; Marie, 76; Ornement Rose, 76; Yellow Hammer, 76

IRIS, varieties of: Alcazar, 26; Beatrice, 26, 192; Blue Beauty, 75; Cherubin, 26; Dark Blue, 75; Florentine, 192; Isolene, 26; King of the Blues and Whites, 75; Lady Sackville, 26; Neglecta, 193; Pallida, 26; Prosper Languier, 26; Queen of May, 193, 245; Rosy Lavender, 75; Seedling Ninety-Two, 26; Souvenir de Zwanenburg ("Mr. Zwanny"), 25, 26, 190, 191, 192; Tenax, 26, 27; Thunderbolt, 75; Trojana, 26; Victor, 26, 192
Irises, enthusiast's information on, 26
Iron sandstone, trees planted over, 192
Isle of Wight Disease, 55, 295
Izzard, Percy, *see* "Countryman's Diary," 141

JAM, recipes for: "Hurts," 270; tomato, 270; rhubarb, 271; marrow, 274
Japonica, 71
Johannesburg, Country Club at, 115

KEATS, 90
King Arthur, garden loved of, 122

LABURNUM, 71, 245
Lavender, 121, 288
Law of trespass, old English, 150
Leaf-buds, checking the formation of, 29

Learning, camera valuable aid to, 39, 40
Lettuce, directions for use of, as vegetable, 275
Life, meaning of, 93
Light, results from denial of, 40
Lilac, varieties of : Louis Spathe, 71 ; Marie-le-Graye, 71 ; Persica, 71
Lilies, varieties of : Auratum, 74 ; Madonna, 74 ; Tiger, 74
Limnanthes Douglassi, 145
Linen, bleaching of, 291
"Little Miss Muffet" : her arrival, 125 ; early life, 126 ; visits the hairdresser, 129 ; her photograph, 130 ; she grows up, 131 ; anxiety concerning her career, 132 ; desire for gardening, 133 ; she goes to college, 134
London : bond slave to, 7 ; compared with New York, 107
Love o' Jove, 245
Lucerne, 162
Lupin, varieties of : Captain, 26 ; Fireflame, 26 ; Zulu, 26

MAETERLINCK, 52, 242
Mahomet, 167
Malus Floribundi, beauty of, 70, 71 ; see also Trees, 22
Manet, 65
Manure : seaweed, 264 ; fish, 264 ; soot, 277 ; burnt refuse, 278
Marrow, see Jam, 274
May, 71
Memories, 95–101
Meredith, George, 36, 287
Merrill : see Californian, 51

Mespilus, bushes of, 146
Michaelmas Daisies, see Asters, 307
Milk, cows', scarcity of, 168 ; substitutes for, 169 ; demand for goats', 171 ; value of goats', 172
Milking-stool, making, 288
Mimosa thorn, 162
Morning Post, the, 79
Morris dancer, 62
Mother Earth, I consecrate myself to, 8
Mouse, my devotion for, 43, 44
Muscari, 27
Muscatel grapes, 162
Myosotis, 71

NATIONAL ARTS CLUB, 106
Nectarines, 162
Nepeta Mussini, 296
Neptune, gardens of, 110
Nurseryman's shop-window, admiration of, 72

OLD PLUM TREE, the, description of, 18 ; fall of, 19 ; child of, 19 ; wizardry of, 19
Orange trees in New South Wales, 273
Orchard grown from pear and apple pips, 30 ; treatment of, 30, 31.
Orchards in : British Columbia, 272 ; Devon, 272 ; Tasmania, 272 ; Worcestershire, 272
Oriental poppies, 25

PACKARD, Mrs. Ardele, 295
Parsnip, maggot pest to, 265 ; only one cure for, 265 ; storing not required, 266

INDEX

Peaches, growing of, with dry subsoil, 30
Pears, growing of, with dry subsoil, 30
Peas, 288
Pegler, Master Holmes, 169, 171, 172, 179; *The Book of the Goat*, 176
" Perry and his Missis," 25
Perry's Hardy Plant Farm, 25
Picnic, the, 79–104
Pineapples in Natal, 273
Playwright, company of a, 24; my escape from, 24; discovered by, 27
Poetry, discussion on, 89–94
Poets, opinion of, 89
Poplars, memories connected with, 283, *see also* Trees, 282
Poppies, dance of, 242
Poppy: Perry's White, 25; birthplace of, 25
Pretoria, streets of, 115

RABBIT, as pet, failure of experiment, 46
Radiculæ, 28
Rambler rose, a happy trick with, 229–30; pruning of, 233; Dorothy Perkins, shoring of, 233
Religion, the best, 12
Rhododendrons, 27, 71
Rhubarb, *see* Jam, 271
Ribbons, varied significance of, 58–62; Ribbon of the Road, 61
Rock plant, description of, 58
Root-pruning, 27; time for, 28, 29
Roots, excessive development of, 28; encouragement of horizontal, 29; surface, 29

Roses, 227–41; varieties of: American Pillar, 235; Aviateur Blériot, 236; Betty, 237; Commander Jules Gravereaux, 240; General MacArthur, 236; Goldfinch, 234; Ideal, 237; Irish Elegance, 237; Juliet, 239; Lady Hillingdon, 236; Los Angeles, 236; Lyon, 237; Madame Abel Chatenay, 237; Magnolia, 239; Mrs. Longworth, 237; Mrs. Massey, 237; Pax, 197; President Bouche (Austrian Copper Briar), 240, 245; Queen Alexandra, 239; Red Letter Day, 240; Robert Craig, 234; Snow Queen, 237; Sunburst, 239; Titania, 240; William Allen, 234
Rose-beds, planning of, 235–37
Rose-beetle, faults of, 241
Rotunda Maternity Hospital, Dublin, my training at, 167
Royal Horticultural Show, 76
Royal Horticultural Society, diploma of, 204

SAGE, how to crop, 275
Sandy soil, phlox grown in, 114
Scott, 177
Sea-anemone, 296
Sea-holly, 297
Seed-bed, making of, 204–207
Service, brother-priests in, 11
Shakespeare, 90
Shrines, description of, 283–86
Silk-making, description of, 62
Snapdragons, 244, 297
Soot, ingredients of, 277

South Africa: envy of, 111; beautiful gardens of, 112; carved designs in Dutch farmhouses, 112; valleys of, 162; ostriches in, 163; vineyards and peach orchards in, 273; the General leaves for, 307
Starlings, 22
Stevenson, R. L., 105, 262
Summer rose, origin of, 34
Syringa, 71

TANGERINE TREES in New South Wales, 273
Tatty-Bogle, 57, 161, 208, 309; Benrimo's devotion to, 248–60
Tea-plant, sprays of, 119
Telham Beauty, see Canterbury Bells
Tennyson, 68, 89, 90, 227; extract from *Locksley Hall*, 89
Thrush, 22
Tit, 22
Tomato, see Jam, 270
Topiary work, 11
Transplanting, time for, 28
Travel diary, extract from, 114

Trees: Almond, 71; Apple, 27, 277; Beech, 18, 244; Birch, 17, 244; Damson, 27; Gooseberry, 27; Larch, 244; *Malus Floribundi*, 22; May, 18; Nut, 32; Plum, 18; Poplar, 282; Thuja, 18
Tritomas, 245
Tulip, varieties of: Bronze Queen, 76; Clara Butt, 77; Couleur Cardinal, 77; Cottage Maid, 76, 77; Don Pedro, 77; The Fawn, 77; Gesneriana Major, 77; Ingelscombe Yellow, 77; La Tristesse, 76; La Tulipe Noire, 77; Moonlight, 76; Zebra, 77

USK, garden overlooking the, 120

VIOLAS, 11

WALLFLOWERS, 146
War-baby, birth of, 64; our care of, 65
Waverley Abbey, 177, 308
Whortleberries, gathering of, 269
Willow Tree, The, 261

Yellow Jacket, The, 10, 261